P9-AGS-419

ISTEP+ Coach
Mathematics
Grade 4

Coach
America's Best for Student Success

Triumph Learning®

Jerome D. Kaplan, Ed.D.

ISTEP+ Coach, Mathematics, Grade 4
163IN
ISBN-10: 1-60471-428-X
ISBN-13: 978-1-60471-428-9

Author: Jerome D. Kaplan, Ed.D.
Cover Image: Indiana has a long and rich auto racing history. © Designpics/Punchstock

Triumph Learning® 136 Madison Avenue, 7th Floor, New York, NY 10016
Kevin McAliley, President and Chief Executive Officer

Table of Contents

To the Student

This book is called the ***ISTEP+ Coach, Mathematics, Grade 4***. It will help you prepare for the ISTEP+ in Mathematics.

Here is how the *ISTEP+ Coach, Mathematics, Grade 4* can help you:

- It shows you what the math questions on the test are like.
- It tells you what you need to know to do well on the test.
- Finally, it gives you practice on the kind of math that will be on the test.

The ISTEP+ Test in Math has many **multiple-choice questions**. They are like the ones you will work with in this book. After each question there are four possible answers. Only one is correct. The others are wrong. You must mark the one correct answer for each question.

The ISTEP+ Test also has **open-ended questions**—short answer questions and questions that require explanations. On these questions, you will have to write your answers in your test booklet as clearly as you can.

Here are some tips that will help when you work in this book and when you take the test:

- Read each question carefully.
- Work as carefully as you can.
- Make sure you answer the question that is asked.
- Ask yourself if the answer makes sense.
- If you cannot decide on the answer to a multiple-choice question, make the best guess you can. There is no penalty for guessing.
- Write clear answers to open-ended questions. Write a full explanation when you are asked to explain your answer.
- Answer as many questions as you can.

Use these tips throughout the book and when you take the test.

Number Sense

1 Place Value and Writing Numbers

4.1.1: Read and write whole numbers up 1,000,000.
4.1.2: Identify and write whole numbers up to 1,000,000, given a place-value model.

This is a place-value chart. It shows the values of each digit of the number 824,517.

hundred thousands	ten thousands	thousands	hundreds	tens	ones
8	2	4	5	1	7

Example 1

What is the value of the 3 in 637,259?

STRATEGY: **Use a place-value chart.**

STEP 1:   Write the digits of 637,259 in the chart.

hundred thousands	ten thousands	thousands	hundreds	tens	ones
6	3	7	2	5	9

STEP 2:   Read the value of 3 from the chart.

SOLUTION: **The value of 3 is 3 ten thousands, or 30,000.**

Example 2

A radio announcer said that there were eighty-five thousand, seven hundred two people at a football game. Write this number in standard form.

STRATEGY: **Read the number to yourself. As you read it, follow the steps below.**

STEP 1:   There are eighty-five thousand. Write 85.

85

STEP 2:   Write a comma to show that 85 refers to thousands.

85,

STEP 3:   Continue reading the number: seven hundred two. Write 702 after the comma.

85,702

SOLUTION: **The number in standard form is 85,702.**

Sample Test Questions

1 What is the value of the 9 in 603,942?

Ⓐ 90,000

Ⓑ 9,000

Ⓒ 900

Ⓓ 90

2 What is the value of the 0 in 706,423?

Ⓐ tens place

Ⓑ hundreds place

Ⓒ thousands place

Ⓓ ten thousands place

3 What number does this tally chart show? (Remember ⩕ = 5)

1,000's	100's	10's	1's
⩕	⩕ IIII	II	⩕ ⩕ IIII

Ⓐ 59,214

Ⓑ 5,934

Ⓒ 5,924

Ⓓ 5,424

4 If ✳ = 1,000, ♣ = 100, and ✦ = 10, what number is represented by the following?

✳ ✳ ✳ ♣ ♣ ♣ ♣ ♣ ♣ ✦ ✦

Ⓐ 362,000

Ⓑ 36,200

Ⓒ 3,620

Ⓓ 362

5 Felix saw a number in a book written this way:

90,000 + 7,000 + 500 + 30 + 8

What is another way to write this number?

Ⓐ 975.38

Ⓑ 97,538

Ⓒ 975,380

Ⓓ 97,000,538

6 What digit is in the thousands place of 465,807?

Ⓐ 4

Ⓑ 5

Ⓒ 6

Ⓓ 8

7 What is the word form of 942,735?

Ⓐ nine hundred forty-two thousand, seven hundred thirty-five

Ⓑ nine hundred forty-two thousand, seven hundred fifty-three

Ⓒ nine hundred forty-two million, seven hundred thirty-five

Ⓓ ninety-four thousand, seven hundred thirty-five

8 Rodney read this number: nine hundred sixty-two thousand, four hundred two. What is Rodney's number in standard form?

_____

9 Elijah described a number this way.

It has 7 hundred thousands.
It has 4 ten thousands
It has 3 hundreds.
It has 9 tens.

What number did Elijah describe?

_____

Explain your answer.

_____

_____

_____

_____

2 Comparing Whole Numbers

4.1.4: Order and compare whole numbers using symbols for "less than" (<), "equal to" (=), and "greater than" (>).

You can use place value to compare and order numbers.

Example 1

Place these numbers in order from least to greatest:

| 33,215 | 35,271 | 33,499 |

STRATEGY: **Use place value.**

STEP 1: Compare the ten thousands places:

| **3**3,215 | **3**5,271 | **3**3,499 |

All three numbers have 3 ten thousands. Therefore, we have to look at the thousands place.

STEP 2: Compare the thousands places:

| 3**3**,215 | 3**5**,271 | 3**3**,499 |

The thousands place of 35,271 is more than the thousands places of both 33,215 and 33,499. So, 35,271 is the greatest.

STEP 3: Compare the hundreds places of the two other numbers:

| 33,**2**15 | 33,**4**99 |

The hundreds place of 33,499 is greater than the hundreds place of 33,215. So, 33,499 is greater than 33,215.

SOLUTION: **The order of the numbers from least to greatest is:**

| **33,215** | **33,499** | **35,271** |

You can compare numbers using symbols.

> means "greater than." For example, 45 > 32.

< means "less than." For example, 56 < 91.

= means "equal to." For example, 67 = 67.

Example 2

What symbol makes this number sentence true?

435 ☐ 657

STRATEGY: **Review the list of symbols.**

STEP 1: > means greater than. 435 is not greater than 675.

STEP 2: < means less than. 435 is less than 675.

SOLUTION: **The symbol that makes the number sentence true is <.**

435 $\boxed{<}$ 675

Sample Test Questions

1 Which set of numbers is in order from least to greatest?

Ⓐ 3,343; 3,243; 2,343

Ⓑ 4,646; 4,666; 4,466

Ⓒ 3,085; 3,805; 3,508

Ⓓ 5,014; 5,104; 5,410

2 If the following numbers were placed in order from greatest to least, which would be second in the series?

256,108   276,112

256,192   592,101

Ⓐ 256,108

Ⓑ 276,112

Ⓒ 256,192

Ⓓ 592,101

3 What symbol makes this number sentence true?

208 ☐ 280

Ⓐ >

Ⓑ +

Ⓒ =

Ⓓ <

4 Put the following days in order from the least to greatest, based on museum attendance.

Day	Museum Attendance
Monday	2,651
Tuesday	2,625
Wednesday	3,302
Thursday	2,598
Friday	2,615

Ⓐ Friday, Monday, Wednesday, Thursday, Tuesday

Ⓑ Thursday, Monday, Wednesday, Tuesday, Friday

Ⓒ Thursday, Friday, Tuesday, Monday, Wednesday

Ⓓ Monday, Wednesday, Friday, Tuesday, Thursday

5 The table shows the four tallest mountains in South America in alphabetical order.

Mountain	Height
Aconcagua	22,834 feet
Bonete	22,546 feet
Ojos del Salado	22,572 feet
Tupungato	22,310 feet

Which mountain is the third tallest?

Ⓐ Aconcagua

Ⓑ Bonete

Ⓒ Ojos del Salado

Ⓓ Tupungato

6 Which number is least?

458,107 438,107
448,107 528,107

Ⓐ 458,107

Ⓑ 438,107

Ⓒ 448,107

Ⓓ 528,107

7 Adam read this sentence:

546 is greater than 203.

What symbol means "greater than"?

Ⓐ >

Ⓑ =

Ⓒ ×

Ⓓ <

8 What symbol completes this number sentence?

10,009 ☐ 10,009

Ⓐ >

Ⓑ =

Ⓒ ×

Ⓒ <

9 What symbol completes this number sentence?

78,605 ☐ 76,508

Ⓐ +

Ⓑ >

Ⓒ <

Ⓓ =

10 Veronica wrote this number sentence. She forgot to include the symbol that would make the number sentence true.

59,602 ☐ 59,620

What symbol makes Veronica's number sentence true?

_____

11 Write these numbers in order from least to greatest.

32,490 41,930 34,903 14,039

_____

3 | Models for Fractions Equal to and Greater Than 1

4.1.5: Rename and rewrite whole numbers as fractions.
4.1.6: Name and write mixed numbers, using objects or pictures.
4.1.7: Name and write mixed numbers as improper fractions, using objects or pictures.

Whole numbers can be shown as fractions.

Example 1

This model shows 3 squares.

How many thirds are equal to 3? Write the answer as a fraction.

STRATEGY: **Divide the squares into thirds.**

STEP 1: Divide each square into thirds by drawing segments.

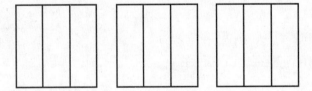

STEP 2: How many thirds are in the 3 squares?

Count the thirds. There are 9 thirds.

STEP 3: Write 9 thirds as a fraction.

Say "9 thirds" and write the fraction you hear.

9 thirds is the same as $\frac{9}{3}$.

SOLUTION: **There are 9 thirds in 3. Write this as $3 = \frac{9}{3}$.**

This diagram shows a fraction greater than 1.

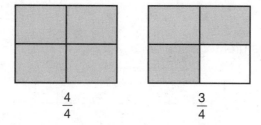

$$\frac{4}{4} \qquad\qquad \frac{3}{4}$$

The rectangles are each divided into 4 equal parts, or fourths.

The two rectangles together show the fraction seven-fourths.

The fraction is written as $\frac{7}{4}$.

If a numerator is greater than its denominator, the fraction is greater than 1.

You can also write $\frac{7}{4}$ as $1\frac{3}{4}$ (one and three-fourths).

$1\frac{3}{4}$ is called a mixed number—it is made up of a whole number and a fraction.

All mixed numbers are greater than 1.

Example 2

Write the mixed number represented by this diagram.

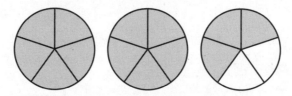

STRATEGY: **Read the whole number part and then read the fraction part.**

STEP 1: Read the whole number part.

The first 2 circles are shaded, so the whole number part is 2.

STEP 2: Read the fraction part.

The third circle shows $\frac{3}{5}$.

STEP 3: Combine the whole number part and the fraction part.

The mixed number is $2\frac{3}{5}$.

Say "two and three-fifths."

SOLUTION: **The diagram shows $2\frac{3}{5}$.**

Example 3

Which of these fractions is greater than 1?

$$\frac{5}{6} \qquad \frac{3}{5} \qquad \frac{3}{2} \qquad \frac{9}{9}$$

STRATEGY: **Compare the numerator and the denominator of each fraction.**

Which fraction has a numerator greater than the denominator?

The numerator of $\frac{3}{2}$ is greater than the denominator.

So, $\frac{3}{2}$ is a fraction greater than 1.

SOLUTION: $\frac{3}{2} > 1$

NOTE: The numerator of $\frac{9}{9}$ equals its denominator. So this fraction is equal to 1.

Sample Test Questions

For Questions 1–3, find the mixed number shown by each model.

1

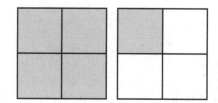

Ⓐ $1\frac{1}{8}$

Ⓑ $1\frac{1}{4}$

Ⓒ $1\frac{1}{2}$

Ⓓ $2\frac{1}{4}$

2

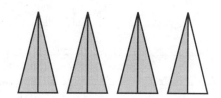

Ⓐ $2\frac{1}{4}$

Ⓑ $3\frac{1}{2}$

Ⓒ $3\frac{3}{4}$

Ⓓ $4\frac{1}{2}$

3

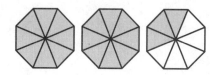

Ⓐ $2\frac{3}{8}$

Ⓑ $2\frac{1}{2}$

Ⓒ $2\frac{3}{4}$

Ⓓ $2\frac{5}{8}$

4 Which model shows $2\frac{1}{4}$?

Ⓐ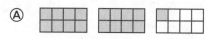

Ⓑ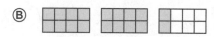

Ⓒ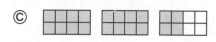

Ⓓ

5 Which number is less than 1?

Ⓐ $2\frac{1}{5}$

Ⓑ $\frac{5}{6}$

Ⓒ $1\frac{1}{10}$

Ⓓ $10\frac{1}{8}$

6 Which number is greater than 1?

Ⓐ $\frac{6}{8}$

Ⓑ $\frac{5}{6}$

Ⓒ $\frac{7}{6}$

Ⓓ $\frac{9}{40}$

7 What fraction is shown by the shaded part of the model?

Ⓐ $\frac{2}{3}$

Ⓑ $\frac{3}{3}$

Ⓒ $\frac{5}{3}$

Ⓓ $\frac{7}{3}$

8 What fraction is shown by the shaded part of the model?

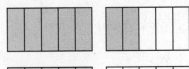

Ⓐ $\frac{12}{5}$

Ⓑ 2

Ⓒ $\frac{7}{5}$

Ⓓ $\frac{5}{5}$

9 Which number is less than 1?

Ⓐ $\frac{10}{9}$

Ⓑ $\frac{8}{9}$

Ⓒ $\frac{9}{7}$

Ⓓ $\frac{11}{10}$

10 Write a fraction equal to 1.

_____

11 Write a fraction equal to 4.

_____

Explain your answer.

_____

_____

_____

_____

4 Decimals

4.1.8: Write tenths and hundredths in decimal and fraction notations. Know the fraction and decimal equivalents for halves and fourths (e.g., $\frac{1}{2} = 0.5 = 0.50$; $\frac{7}{4} = 1\frac{3}{4} = 1.75$).

The decimal 0.25 is equivalent to $\frac{1}{4}$. (Equivalent is another way of saying "means the same as.")

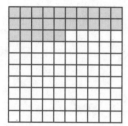

The decimal 0.5 is equivalent to $\frac{1}{2}$.

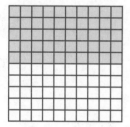

The decimal 0.75 is equivalent to $\frac{3}{4}$.

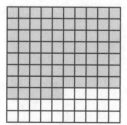

The decimal 0.4 is equivalent to $\frac{4}{10}$.

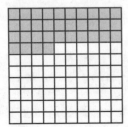

The decimal 0.34 is equivalent to $\frac{34}{100}$.

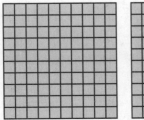

The decimal 2.51 is equivalent to $2\frac{51}{100}$.

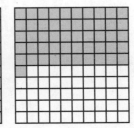

Example 1

What is the decimal name for the shaded part of this figure?

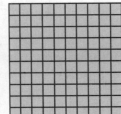

STRATEGY: **Write the fraction.**

STEP 1: Write the fraction for the shaded part.

$$\frac{\text{number of shaded parts}}{\text{total number of parts}} = \frac{9}{10}$$

STEP 2: Write the decimal for the fraction $\frac{9}{10}$.

SOLUTION: **The decimal for $\frac{9}{10}$ is 0.9.**

Example 2

Write the decimal represented by the shaded parts of the grids.

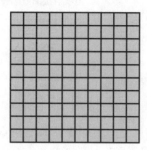 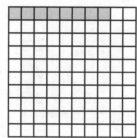

STRATEGY: **Write the mixed number. Then write an equivalent decimal.**

STEP 1: Write the mixed number.

The shaded parts show 1 whole and $\frac{8}{100}$, or $1\frac{8}{100}$.

STEP 2: Write the decimal for $1\frac{8}{100}$.

SOLUTION: **The decimal for $1\frac{8}{100}$ is 1.08.**

Example 3

What is the value of the 7 in 1.75?

STRATEGY: **Use a place-value chart.**

STEP 1: Write 1.75 in a place value chart.

ones	.	tenths	hundredths
1	.	7	5

STEP 2: Read the value of the 7 from the chart.

SOLUTION: **The value of the 7 is 7 tenths, or 0.7.**

Sample Test Questions

1 Choose the decimal represented by the shaded parts of the grids.

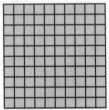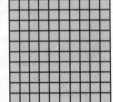

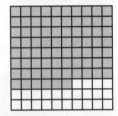

Ⓐ 2.67

Ⓑ 2.76

Ⓒ 2.86

Ⓓ 27.6

2 Stephanie carried a package weighing 9.23 pounds. What is the value of the 3?

Ⓐ 3

Ⓑ 0.3

Ⓒ 0.03

Ⓒ 0.003

3 Maria ate $3\frac{3}{4}$ pieces of pizza. Which decimal shows the amount of pizza Maria ate?

Ⓐ 3.25 pieces

Ⓑ 3.34 pieces

Ⓒ 3.75 pieces

Ⓓ 37.5 pieces

4 Linea wrote this mixed number.

$$4\frac{92}{100}$$

Which decimal shows Linea's mixed number?

Ⓐ 492.100

Ⓑ 49.21

Ⓒ 4.92

Ⓓ 4.29

5 What is the value of the 4 in 85.64?

Ⓐ 4 hundreds

Ⓑ 4 tens

Ⓒ 4 tenths

Ⓓ 4 hundredths

6 Which decimal is the same as $34\frac{1}{2}$?

   Ⓐ 34.12

   Ⓑ 34.25

   Ⓒ 34.5

   Ⓓ 34.75

7 How can you write the sum of these numbers?

> 8 tenths
>
> 2 tens
>
> 1 hundredths
>
> 3 ones

   Ⓐ 2.381

   Ⓑ 23.81

   Ⓒ 238.1

   Ⓓ 2,381

8 Which decimal is the same as $5\frac{5}{100}$?

   Ⓐ 5.5

   Ⓑ 5.05

   Ⓒ 5.005

   Ⓓ 55.0

9 Which decimal is the same as $54\frac{8}{100}$?

   Ⓐ 54.8100

   Ⓑ 54.88

   Ⓒ 54.8

   Ⓓ 54.08

10 Magda wrote this fraction.

$$54\frac{78}{100}$$

What is the decimal form of Magda's fraction?

_____

Explain your answer.

_____

_____

_____

_____

11 Shade the grids to show 2.65.

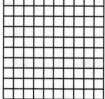

5 Rounding to the Nearest 10, 100, and 1,000

4.1.3: Round whole numbers up to 10,000 to the nearest ten, hundred, and thousand.

Rounding to the Nearest 10

Example 1

Round 67 to the nearest 10.

STRATEGY: **Follow these steps.**

> **STEP 1:** Place 67 on a number line.
>
>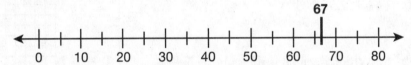
>
> **STEP 2:** Determine whether 67 is closer to 60 or 70.
>
> 67 is closer to 70, so round UP.

SOLUTION: **67 rounds up to 70.**

Example 2

Round 35 to the nearest 10.

STRATEGY: **Use a number line.**

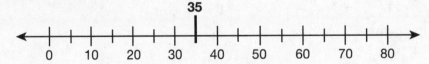

35 is halfway between 30 and 40. When this happens, round UP.

SOLUTION: **35 rounds up to 40.**

Rounding to the Nearest 100

Example 3

Round 417 to the nearest 100.

STRATEGY: **Use a number line.**

Is 417 closer to 400 or 500?

SOLUTION: **Since 417 is closer to 400 than 500, round DOWN to 400.**

> **NOTE:** How would you round 450? Since it is halfway between 400 and 500, you would round up to 500.

Rounding to the Nearest 1,000

Example 4

Round 5,500 to the nearest 1,000.

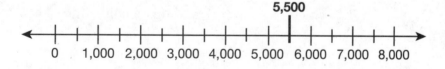

STRATEGY: **Use the number-line strategy.**

5,500 is halfway between 5,000 and 6,000.

When a number ends in 500, round UP.

SOLUTION: **5,500 rounds up to 6,000.**

Sample Test Questions

1 A new TV set is advertised at $424. Round this price to the nearest $10.

Ⓐ $400

Ⓑ $410

Ⓒ $420

Ⓓ $430

2 The distance from John's house to his grandparents' house is 114 miles. About how many miles is this distance? (Round the distance to the nearest 100 miles.)

Ⓐ 200 miles

Ⓑ 150 miles

Ⓒ 100 miles

Ⓓ 50 miles

3 Which number, when rounded to the nearest 100, does not round to 500?

Ⓐ 451

Ⓑ 490

Ⓒ 524

Ⓓ 550

4 Stan's bill at a bicycle shop came to $73.24. The shop owner rounded the amount to the nearest $10. What is true about the rounded amount?

Ⓐ It is less than $73.24.

Ⓑ It is more than $73.24.

Ⓒ It is exactly equal to $73.24.

Ⓓ It is $10 less than $73.24.

5 Mark counted 4,803 tickets sold for the Fall Festival. Round this figure to the nearest 100.

Ⓐ 5,000

Ⓑ 4,900

Ⓒ 4,800

Ⓓ 4,000

6 Round 2,500 to the nearest 1,000.

Ⓐ 2,000

Ⓑ 2,600

Ⓒ 2,900

Ⓓ 3,000

7 Round 2,555 to the nearest 100.

Ⓐ 2,500

Ⓑ 2,600

Ⓒ 2,700

Ⓓ 3,000

8 Round 8,502 to the nearest thousand.

_____

Explain your answer.

_____

_____

_____

_____

_____

9 Round 4,467 to the nearest ten.

_____

6 Rounding Decimals

4.1.9: Round two-place decimals to tenths or to the nearest whole number.

Rounding to the Nearest Whole Number

Example 1

A living room is 4.7 meters long. Round 4.7 meters to the nearest whole number.

STRATEGY: **Find the whole number 4.7 is closest to.**

STEP 1:   Place 4.7 on a number line.

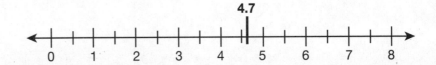

STEP 2:   Is 4.7 closer to 4 or 5?

4.7 is closer to 5.

SOLUTION: **4.7 rounded to the nearest whole number is 5. The living room is about 5 meters long.**

Example 2

Paul took 17.5 hours to finish a project at work. Round 17.5 to the nearest whole number.

STRATEGY: **Use the following rule.**

> **If a number is exactly halfway between two whole numbers, round UP.**

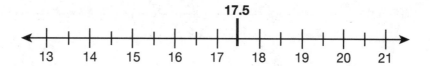

17.5 is halfway between 17 and 18.

Round up to 18.

SOLUTION: **17.5 rounded to the nearest whole number is 18. So, Paul took about 18 hours to finish the project.**

Example 3

Leah's dog weighs 9.83 kg. Round 9.83 to the nearest tenth of a kilogram.

STRATEGY: **Find the tenth that 9.83 is closest to.**

STEP 1: Place 9.83 on a number line.

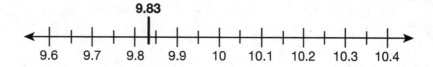

STEP 2: Is 9.83 closer to 9.8 or 9.9?

9.83 is closer to 9.8.

SOLUTION: **9.83 kg rounds to 9.8 kg. Leah's dog weighs about 9.8 kg.**

Example 4

A pencil measures 7.45 inches long. Round 7.45 to the nearest tenth of an inch.

STRATEGY: **Use the following rule.**

> **If a number is exactly halfway between two tenths, round UP.**

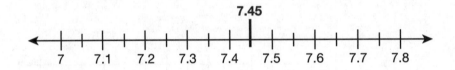

7.45 is halfway between 7.4 and 7.5.

SOLUTION: **7.45 inches rounds to 7.5 inches. The pencil is about 7.5 inches long.**

Sample Test Questions

1 Julie traveled 65.5 miles to get to the stadium. Round the distance to the nearest whole number.

Ⓐ 60 miles

Ⓑ 65 miles

Ⓒ 66 miles

Ⓓ 70 miles

2 A table is 1.76 meters long. Round the length to the nearest whole number.

Ⓐ 1 meter

Ⓑ 1.7 meters

Ⓒ 1.8 meters

Ⓓ 2 meters

3 Round 87.59 to the nearest tenth.

Ⓐ 87.7

Ⓑ 87.6

Ⓒ 87.5

Ⓓ 87.4

4 Five kilometers is about 3.1 miles. Which of these numbers rounds to 3.1?

Ⓐ 3.21

Ⓑ 3.15

Ⓒ 3.12

Ⓓ 3.04

5 Miguel swam a lap in 1.28 minutes. Round Miguel's time to the nearest tenth of a minute.

Ⓐ 1 minute

Ⓑ 1.2 minutes

Ⓒ 1.25 minutes

Ⓓ 1.3 minutes

6 Phil watched TV for 6.25 hours last weekend. Round this time to the nearest whole number.

Ⓐ 6 hours

Ⓑ 6.5 hours

Ⓒ 7 hours

Ⓓ 10 hours

7 Paula's long jump record is 7.64 feet. Round this length to the nearest tenth of a foot.

Ⓐ 7 feet

Ⓑ 7.6 feet

Ⓒ 7.7 feet

Ⓓ 8 feet

8 Therese wrote a decimal that can be rounded to 45.6. Write three decimals that will round to 45.6.

☐☐ . ☐☐

☐☐ . ☐☐

☐☐ . ☐☐

Use what you know about rounding decimals to explain why the decimals you wrote are correct.

_____

_____

_____

_____

_____

Progress Check for Lessons 1–6

1 If the following numbers were ordered from greatest to least, which would be second in the series?

67,108 76,108
67,192 69,108

(A) 67,108

(B) 76,108

(C) 67,192

(D) 69,108

2 What fraction is shown by the shaded parts of the model?

 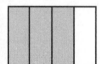

(A) $\frac{3}{4}$

(B) $\frac{4}{4}$

(C) $\frac{5}{4}$

(D) $\frac{7}{4}$

3 85,452 people bought tickets to Jefferson High School's football games last year. How do you read this number?

(A) eighty-five thousand, four hundred fifty

(B) eighty-five ten thousand, four hundred fifty-two

(C) eighty-five thousand, four hundred fifty-two

(D) eighty-five thousand, four thousand fifty-two

4 What is the value of 8 in 38,621?

(A) 800

(B) 8,000

(C) 80,000

(D) 800,000

5 If you are rounding to the nearest 1,000, which number does not round to 57,000?

(A) 56,587

(B) 56,940

(C) 57,307

(D) 57,500

6 What decimal is the same as $4\frac{9}{100}$?

Ⓐ 4.009

Ⓑ 4.09

Ⓒ 4.90

Ⓓ 4.9

7 Choose the decimal represented by the shaded parts of the grids.

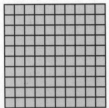 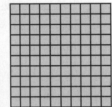

Ⓐ 0.028

Ⓑ 0.28

Ⓒ 2.08

Ⓓ 2.8

8 Which number rounds to 2?

Ⓐ 1.75

Ⓑ 2.75

Ⓒ 1.45

Ⓓ 2.55

9 Which symbol makes this number sentence true?

9,806 ☐ 9,680

Ⓐ −

Ⓑ =

Ⓒ >

Ⓓ <

10 Which decimal rounds to 54.4?

Ⓐ 54.37

Ⓑ 54.34

Ⓒ 54.46

Ⓓ 54.64

11 Round 9,408 to the nearest ten.

Ⓐ 9,000

Ⓑ 9,400

Ⓒ 9,410

Ⓓ 9,420

12 Which decimal is the same as $32\frac{3}{4}$?

Ⓐ 32.25

Ⓑ 32.34

Ⓒ 32.65

Ⓓ 32.75

36

13 Esteban wrote this number.

347,091

What is the value of the 4 in Esteban's number?

Ⓐ 4 hundred thousands

Ⓑ 4 ten thousands

Ⓒ 4 thousands

Ⓓ 4 hundreds

14 Which decimal rounds to 87?

Ⓐ 87.7

Ⓑ 87.17

Ⓒ 86.4

Ⓓ 86.17

15 Judy wrote this number.

38,192

What is Judy's number rounded to the nearest thousand?

Ⓐ 30,000

Ⓑ 35,000

Ⓒ 38,000

Ⓓ 39,000

16 What fraction is shown by the shaded parts of the model?

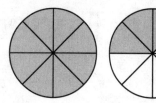

Ⓐ $\frac{8}{11}$

Ⓑ $\frac{4}{8}$

Ⓒ $\frac{6}{8}$

Ⓓ $\frac{11}{8}$

17 Which is a true number sentence?

Ⓐ 786 < 768

Ⓑ 365 > 398

Ⓒ 908 < 980

Ⓓ 607 > 657

18 Which is another name for 2?

Ⓐ $\frac{1}{2}$

Ⓑ $\frac{4}{2}$

Ⓒ $\frac{5}{2}$

Ⓓ $\frac{2}{2}$

Standard 1: Number Sense
Open-Ended Questions

1   a)   Choose a number greater than 10,000 and less than 999,999. The number you choose must include at least 3 different digits.

_____

b)   Write the number in expanded form (for example, 12,418 would be 10,000 + 2,000 + 400 + 10 + 8).

_____

c)   Using the symbols below, write your number.

     a = 100,000   c = 1,000   e = 10

     b = 10,000   d = 100   f = 1

_____

2   Use these rectangles to show $\frac{6}{4}$.

Explain your answer.

_____

_____

_____

3   Kate rounded a 2-digit number and got 80. Write all the numbers that she could have started with.

_____

_____

_____

_____

4   Mike started with a decimal in hundredths. After he rounded his number to the nearest tenth, he got 8.4. Write five decimals he could have started with.

_____

_____

Computation

7 | Adding and Subtracting Whole Numbers to 100,000

4.2.1: Understand and use standard algorithms for addition and subtraction.

This lesson gives you more practice in adding and subtracting whole numbers. Here are two examples that show regrouping.

Example 1

16,587 + 48,249 = ?

STRATEGY: **Make sure the digits are lined up, and don't forget to regroup.**

STEP 1: Write the numbers vertically so the same places are lined up.

```
  16587
+ 48249
```

STEP 2: Add the ones, making sure to regroup.

7 + 9 = 16

Regroup 16 as 1 ten and 6 ones.

```
      1
  16587
+ 48249
_____
      6
```

STEP 3: Add column by column, regrouping where necessary.

```
  1 11
  16587
+ 48249
_____
  64836
```

SOLUTION: **The sum is 64,836.**

Example 2

81,925 − 28,408 = ?

STRATEGY: **Follow these steps.**

STEP 1: Write the numbers vertically so the places are lined up.

$$
\begin{array}{r}
81925 \\
-\ 28408 \\
\end{array}
$$

STEP 2: Subtract the ones, making sure to regroup.

Regroup the 2 tens as 1 ten and 10 ones.

$$
\begin{array}{r}
1\,1 \\
819\cancel{2}5 \\
-\ 28408 \\
\hline
7 \\
\end{array}
$$

STEP 3: Subtract column by column, regrouping where necessary.

$$
\begin{array}{r}
71\ \ 11 \\
\cancel{8}19\cancel{2}5 \\
-\ 28408 \\
\hline
53517 \\
\end{array}
$$

SOLUTION: **The difference is 53,517.**

Sample Test Questions

1 45,205 + 3,917 = ?

  Ⓐ 48,112

  Ⓑ 48,122

  Ⓒ 49,112

  Ⓓ 49,122

2 12,581 − 6,347 = ?

  Ⓐ 6,144

  Ⓑ 6,234

  Ⓒ 6,244

  Ⓓ 6,246

3 41,907 + 56,213 = ?

  Ⓐ 97,110

  Ⓑ 97,120

  Ⓒ 98,110

  Ⓓ 98,120

4 47,163 − 8,892 = ?

  Ⓐ 38,271

  Ⓑ 38,361

  Ⓒ 38,371

  Ⓓ 39,371

5 26,306 + 62,914 = ?

  Ⓐ 89,220

  Ⓑ 89,219

  Ⓒ 88,220

  Ⓓ 88,219

6 94,902 − 84,407 = ?

  Ⓐ 10,405

  Ⓑ 10,495

  Ⓒ 10,505

  Ⓓ 10,595

7 7,820 − 2,301 = ?

  Ⓐ 5,421

  Ⓑ 5,519

  Ⓒ 5,521

  Ⓓ 5,529

8 22,604 + 15,387 = ?

  Ⓐ 37,991

  Ⓑ 37,981

  Ⓒ 37,891

  Ⓓ 27,991

9 Find the sum of 68,349 and 21,753.

Show your work.

8 Multiplication and Division Facts

4.2.4: Demonstrate mastery of the multiplication tables for numbers between 1 and 10 and of the corresponding division facts.

4.3.6: Recognize and apply the relationships between addition and multiplication, between subtraction and division, and the inverse relationship between multiplication and division to solve problems.

You need to know the multiplication table up to 10×10.

Example 1

$7 \times 9 = \boxed{}$

STRATEGY: **Use a multiplication table.**

X	0	1	2	3	4	5	6	7	8	9	10
0	0	0	0	0	0	0	0	0	0	0	0
1	0	1	2	3	4	5	6	7	8	9	10
2	0	2	4	6	8	10	12	14	16	18	20
3	0	3	6	9	12	15	18	21	24	27	30
4	0	4	8	12	16	20	24	28	32	36	40
5	0	5	10	15	20	25	30	35	40	45	50
6	0	6	12	18	24	30	36	42	48	54	60
7	0	7	14	21	28	35	42	49	56	(63)	70
8	0	8	16	24	32	40	48	56	64	72	80
9	0	9	18	27	36	45	54	63	72	81	90
10	0	10	20	30	40	50	60	70	80	90	100

STEP 1: Find 7 along the left border of the table.

45

	STEP 2:	Find 9 along the top border of the table.
	STEP 3:	Move your finger from 7 across the table until you are under the 9.
		Follow the paths on the table.
	STEP 4:	What is the number?
		The number where the two paths meet is 63.

SOLUTION: $7 \times 9 = 63$

You can use the chart to find multiplication facts, but you should know the multiplication facts so well that you do not need a chart.

Example 2

Show that $7 \times 9 = 9 \times 7$ by using the chart.

STRATEGY: **Use the diagonal line you see in the chart.**

STEP 1: Follow the steps of Example 1 to find 7×9.

$7 \times 9 = 63$

This number is in a circle.

STEP 2: Use those same steps to find 9×7.

Start at 9. Move your finger from 9 on the left border across the table until you are under the 7. The number under 7 is 63; $9 \times 7 = 63$.

This number is in a square.

STEP 3: Compare the 63 in the circle and the 63 in the square.

These are on opposite sides of the diagonal line.

SOLUTION: $7 \times 9 = 9 \times 7$

The order of numbers in a multiplication fact doesn't change the answer.

> **NOTE:** When learning multiplication, learn half of the facts, the facts above the diagonal line or below it. The other half is the same, with the numbers reversed. Always make sure you learn the facts on the diagonal as well.

You can use multiplication facts to help you learn division facts.

$$21 \div 7 = \boxed{} \quad \Longrightarrow \quad \text{What number, multiplied by 7, equals 21?}$$

The answer is 3 because $7 \times 3 = 21$.

Division is the inverse operation of multiplication.

The numbers 3, 7, and 21 form a multiplication-division fact family.

$$3 \times 7 = 21 \qquad\qquad 7 \times 3 = 21$$

$$21 \div 7 = 3 \qquad\qquad 21 \div 3 = 7$$

or   or

$$21 \div 7 = 3 \qquad\qquad 21 \div 3 = 7$$

Example 3

What other facts are in the fact family of $7 \times 6 = 42$?

STRATEGY: **Use the three numbers to find three other facts.**

STEP 1:   Use the three numbers of $7 \times 6 = 42$ to form a fact family.
The numbers are {6, 7, 42}.

STEP 2:   Write a new multiplication fact and two division facts using the numbers of the fact family.

SOLUTION: **$6 \times 7 = 42$; $42 \div 6 = 7$; $42 \div 7 = 6$**

Example 4

$12 \times 3 = 36$
$36 \div 3 = ?$

STRATEGY: **Remember that multiplication and division are inverse operations.**

$36 \div 3$ asks: What number multiplies 3 to equal 36?

Since $12 \times 3 = 36$, then $36 \div 3 = 12$

SOLUTION: **$36 \div 3 = 12$**

Sample Test Questions

1. $8 \times 7 = \square$
    - (A) 56
    - (B) 63
    - (C) 64
    - (D) 72

2. $9 \times 4 = \square$
    - (A) 18
    - (B) 24
    - (C) 36
    - (D) 48

3. $3 \times 12 = \square$
    - (A) 32
    - (B) 34
    - (C) 36
    - (D) 48

4. $11 \times 8 = \square$
    - (A) 88
    - (B) 87
    - (C) 86
    - (D) 77

5. $7 \times 6 = \square$
    - (A) 42
    - (B) 46
    - (C) 48
    - (D) 54

6. $5 \times 9 = \square$
    - (A) 45
    - (B) 47
    - (C) 49
    - (D) 59

7. $10 \times 7 = \square$
    - (A) 60
    - (B) 70
    - (C) 77
    - (D) 80

8. $12 \times 12 = \square$
    - (A) 12
    - (B) 24
    - (C) 132
    - (D) 144

9 Which fact belongs to the same family as $8 \times 5 = 40$?

ⓐ $45 \div 5 = 9$

ⓑ $36 \div 4 = 9$

ⓒ $40 \div 5 = 8$

ⓓ $48 \div 6 = 8$

10 Which fact belongs to the same family as $34 \div 4 = 8$?

ⓐ $4 \times 4 = 16$

ⓑ $8 \times 4 = 32$

ⓒ $\frac{16}{2} = 8$

ⓓ $\frac{32}{2} = 16$

11 Which fact belongs to the same family as $40 \div 5 = 8$?

ⓐ $5 \times 5 = 25$

ⓑ $\frac{16}{8} = 2$

ⓒ $\frac{40}{2} = 20$

ⓓ $\frac{40}{8} = 5$

12 $7 \times 8 = \square$

ⓐ 45

ⓑ 56

ⓒ 63

ⓓ 66

13 $24 \div 3 = \square$

ⓐ 8

ⓑ 9

ⓒ 12

ⓓ 14

14 $72 \div 8 = \square$

ⓐ 6

ⓑ 7

ⓒ 8

ⓓ 9

15 $49 \div 7 = \square$

ⓐ 5

ⓑ 6

ⓒ 7

ⓓ 8

16 $27 \div 9 = \square$

ⓐ 3

ⓑ 4

ⓒ 6

ⓓ 8

17 $45 \div 5 = \square$

ⓐ 5

ⓑ 9

ⓒ 12

ⓓ 15

18 $35 \div 5 =$ ☐

Ⓐ 4

Ⓑ 5

Ⓒ 6

Ⓓ 7

19 $54 \div 6 =$ ☐

Ⓐ 6

Ⓑ 7

Ⓒ 8

Ⓓ 9

20 $6 \times 8 = 48$

Which of the following is true?

Ⓐ $48 \div 6 = 6$

Ⓑ $48 \div 9 = 6$

Ⓒ $48 \div 8 = 6$

Ⓓ $48 \div 8 = 4$

21 $11 \times 8 = 88$

Which of the following is true?

Ⓐ $\frac{88}{11} = 8$

Ⓑ $\frac{88}{8} = 12$

Ⓒ $\frac{88}{11} = 77$

Ⓓ $\frac{88}{8} = 82$

22 $96 \div 12 = 8$

Which of the following is true?

Ⓐ $8 \times 12 = 76$

Ⓑ $8 \times 14 = 96$

Ⓒ $8 \times 12 = 96$

Ⓓ $8 \times 11 = 92$

23   Write a multiplication fact. Write the other three members of the multiplication-division fact family.

_____

_____

_____

_____

9 Representing Multiplication and Division

4.2.2: Represent as multiplication any situation involving repeated addition.
4.2.3: Represent as division any situation involving the sharing of objects or the number of groups of shared objects.

You can use multiplication to solve a problem that involves repeated addition.

There are 6 children at a party. Each child eats 2 pieces of birthday cake. How many pieces of cake were eaten in all?

You can solve the problem with repeated addition.

$2 + 2 + 2 + 2 + 2 + 2 = 12$ pieces of cake

Or you can solve it with multiplication.

$6 \times 2 = 12$ pieces of cake

Example 1

Mrs. Ramirez gave 3 pencils to each student in her class. There are 23 students in her class. How many pencils did Mrs. Ramirez give out altogether?

STRATEGY: **Use multiplication to solve the problem.**

STEP 1:   Write the factors in the multiplication problem.

The factors that you will multiply are 3 and 23.

STEP 2:   Multiply.

$23 \times 3 = 69$

SOLUTION: **Mrs. Ramirez gave out 69 pencils altogether.**

You can use division to solve problems that involve sharing or separating into equal groups.

Matt has 12 baseball cards. He wants to put them in 4 equal groups. How many cards will Matt put in each group?

Divide 12 by 4.

12 ÷ 4 = 3 cards in each group

Example 2

A clown at a carnival has 27 balloons. He wants to give them out equally to 9 children. How many balloons will each child get?

STRATEGY: **Use division to solve the problem.**

        STEP 1:   Write the division problem.

$$\frac{27}{9} = ?$$

        STEP 2:   Solve.

$$\frac{27}{9} = 3$$

SOLUTION: **Each child will get 3 balloons.**

Sample Test Questions

1 Yuri has 42 pieces of candy. He has 6 bags. How many pieces of candy will Yuri put in each bag if he puts an equal number in each one?

Ⓐ 36 pieces

Ⓑ 12 pieces

Ⓒ 7 pieces

Ⓓ 6 pieces

2 Carolina works at a pet store. A shipment of 21 hamsters arrives. Carolina can only put 3 hamsters in a cage. How many cages does Carolina need?

Ⓐ 3 cages

Ⓑ 5 cages

Ⓒ 7 cages

Ⓓ 9 cages

3 Mr. Clayton is planting his garden. There are 4 rows in his garden. Mr. Clayton will plant 7 lettuce plants in each row. How many lettuce plants will Mr. Clayton plant all together?

Ⓐ 35 plants

Ⓑ 28 plants

Ⓒ 11 plants

Ⓓ 7 plants

4 Harmony is planning a party. She has invited 30 guests. There will be 6 tables at the party. Harmony wants an equal number of guests at each table. How many guests will sit at each table?

Ⓐ 36 guests

Ⓑ 24 guests

Ⓒ 12 guests

Ⓓ 5 guests

5 Iman reads 4 books a week. She has read every week for the past 20 weeks. How many books has Iman read?

Ⓐ 16 books

Ⓑ 24 books

Ⓒ 56 books

Ⓓ 80 books

6 Nicole runs 6 days each week. She runs 12 miles each morning. How many miles does Nicole run in a week?

Ⓐ 2 miles

Ⓑ 36 miles

Ⓒ 48 miles

Ⓓ 72 miles

7 The 4 fifth grade classes at Morris Elementary School are going on a field trip. There are 22 students in each class. How many students are going on the field trip?

8 Write a sentence describing a situation that you (or someone in your family) might be part of that involves repeated addition.

_____

_____

_____

_____

10 Multiplying By One-Digit Whole Numbers

4.2.5: Use a standard algorithm to multiply numbers up to 100 by numbers up to 10, using relevant properties of the number system.

You often need to regroup when you multiply by one-digit whole numbers.

Example 1

$29 \times 7 = ?$

STRATEGY: **Regroup.**

STEP 1: Multiply 7 by the digit in the ones column.

$$\begin{array}{r} 29 \\ \times\ 7 \\ \hline \end{array} \qquad 7 \times 9 = 63$$

Regroup 63 as 6 tens and 3 ones.

Write 3 in the ones column of the answer frame and write 6 in the tens column above the 2.

$$\begin{array}{r} {}^{6} \\ 29 \\ \times\ 7 \\ \hline 3 \end{array}$$

STEP 2: Multiply 7 by the tens digit (2) of the top number.

$7 \times 2 \text{ (tens)} = 14 \text{ (tens)}$

Add the 6 regrouped tens.

$14 \text{ (tens)} + 6 \text{ (tens)} = 20 \text{ (tens)}$

STEP 3:   Write 20 in the answer.

$$
\begin{array}{r}
6 \\
29 \\
\times\ 7 \\
\hline
\mathbf{203}
\end{array}
$$

SOLUTION: **The product is 203.**

Example 2

$52 \times 6 = ?$

STRATEGY: **Regroup.**

STEP 1:   Multiply the ones.

$$
\begin{array}{r}
52 \\
\times\ 6 \\
\hline
\end{array}
\qquad 6 \times 2 = 12
$$

Regroup 12 as 1 ten and 2 ones.

Write 2 in the ones column of the answer frame and write 1 in the tens place above the 5.

$$
\begin{array}{r}
\mathbf{1} \\
52 \\
\times\ 6 \\
\hline
\mathbf{2}
\end{array}
$$

STEP 2:   Multiply 6 by the digit (5) in the tens place.

$6 \times 5 = 30$ (tens)

Add the 1 ten above the 5.

$30 + 1 = 31$ (tens)

Think of 31 tens as 310, or 3 hundreds and 1 ten.

STEP 3:   Complete writing the product.

$$
\begin{array}{r}
1 \\
52 \\
\times\ 6 \\
\hline
\mathbf{312}
\end{array}
$$

SOLUTION: **The product is 312.**

Sample Test Questions

1 $81 \times 2 = ?$

Ⓐ 162

Ⓑ 172

Ⓒ 182

Ⓓ 192

2 $5 \times 94 = ?$

Hint: Change the order of the factors.

$$\begin{array}{r} 94 \\ \times\ 5 \\ \hline \end{array}$$

Ⓐ 450

Ⓑ 470

Ⓒ 490

Ⓓ 510

3 $87 \times 7 = ?$

Ⓐ 569

Ⓑ 589

Ⓒ 609

Ⓓ 669

4 $73 \times 9 = ?$

Ⓐ 81

Ⓑ 637

Ⓒ 647

Ⓓ 657

5 $6 \times 53 = ?$

Ⓐ 338

Ⓑ 328

Ⓒ 318

Ⓓ 308

6 $27 \times 4 = ?$

Ⓐ 108

Ⓑ 118

Ⓒ 128

Ⓓ 138

7 Javier needs to find a product: 76×5.

Here is his calculation.

$$\begin{array}{r} 76 \\ \times\ 5 \\ \hline 350 \end{array}$$

Find and correct his error.

_____

_____

_____

11 Introduction to Long Division

4.2.6: Use a standard algorithm to divide numbers up to 100 by numbers up to 10 without remainders, using relevant properties of the number system.

Quotient
Divisor)Dividend

Example

Find the quotient.

7)84   This means divide 84 by 7.

STRATEGY: **Follow these steps to divide.**

STEP 1:   Estimate the first digit of the quotient.

How many 7's in 8?

Answer: 1

Write 1 above the 8.

$$\frac{1}{7)\overline{84}}$$

STEP 2:   Multiply 1 by the divisor (7) and write the product under 8.

$$\begin{array}{r} 1 \\ 7)\overline{84} \\ 7 \end{array}$$

STEP 3:   Subtract the product of Step 2 from 8.

$$
\begin{array}{r}
1 \\
7\overline{)84} \\
-\ 7 \\
\hline
1
\end{array}
$$

STEP 4:   Bring down the next digit of the dividend (4).

$$
\begin{array}{r}
1 \\
7\overline{)84} \\
-\ 7 \\
\hline
14
\end{array}
$$

STEP 5:   Repeat the procedure in Steps 1 through 4.

$$
\begin{array}{r}
12 \\
7\overline{)84} \\
-\ 7 \\
\hline
14 \\
-\ 14 \\
\hline
0
\end{array}
$$

SOLUTION: **The quotient is 12.**

NOTE: All division problems can be done by following the steps in this example.

Sample Test Questions

1   Divide 96 by 8.

    Ⓐ 10

    Ⓑ 11

    Ⓒ 12

    Ⓓ 13

2 $5\overline{)90}$

    Ⓐ 15

    Ⓑ 16

    Ⓒ 17

    Ⓓ 18

3 $7\overline{)77}$

    Ⓐ 12

    Ⓑ 11

    Ⓒ 10

    Ⓓ 9

4   Divide 99 by 9.

    Ⓐ 12

    Ⓑ 11

    Ⓒ 10

    Ⓓ 9

5   Divide 84 by 6.

    Ⓐ 11

    Ⓑ 12

    Ⓒ 13

    Ⓓ 14

6   Divide 68 by 4.

    Ⓐ 15

    Ⓑ 17

    Ⓒ 19

    Ⓓ 21

7 $3\overline{)87}$

    Ⓐ 31

    Ⓑ 29

    Ⓒ 27

    Ⓓ 25

8 $6\overline{)90}$

    Ⓐ 10

    Ⓑ 15

    Ⓒ 20

    Ⓓ 25

9   Find the quotient. Show your work.

    656 divided by 8

_____

12 The Properties of 0 and 1 in Multiplication and Division

4.2.7: Understand the special properties of 0 and 1 in multiplication and division.

The properties of 0 and 1 can help you solve multiplication and division problems.

Multiplying by 1

A number multiplied by 1 is equal to the number.

$$176 \times 1 = 176$$

Multiplying by 0

A number multiplied by 0 equals 0.

$$843 \times 0 = 0$$

Dividing by 1

A number divided by 1 is equal to the number.

$$\frac{921}{1} = 921$$

Dividing by 0

Dividing by 0 is impossible.

$\frac{38}{0}$ is impossible.

Example 1

What number makes this sentence true?

$$\frac{205}{\Box} = 205$$

STRATEGY: **Look at the properties above.**

Dividing a number by 1 gives the number.

SOLUTION: **1 makes the sentence true.**
$$\frac{205}{1} = 205$$

Example 2

What symbol makes this sentence true?

4,729 $\Box$ 0 = 0

STRATEGY: **Look at the properties above.**

Multiplying a number by 0 gives 0.

SOLUTION: **The symbol is ×. 4,729 × 0 = 0.**

Sample Test Questions

Choose the number that makes the sentence true.

1 $45 \times 1 = \boxed{}$

Ⓐ 1

Ⓑ 44

Ⓒ 45

Ⓓ 46

2 $\boxed{} \times 1 = 378$

Ⓐ 0

Ⓑ 1

Ⓒ 377

Ⓓ 378

3 $\frac{603}{1} = \boxed{}$

Ⓐ 604

Ⓑ 603

Ⓒ 602

Ⓓ 1

4 $\frac{23}{0} = \boxed{}$

Ⓐ impossible

Ⓑ 23

Ⓒ 1

Ⓓ 0

5 $200 \times \boxed{} = 200$

Ⓐ 0   Ⓓ 200

Ⓑ 1   Ⓒ 199

6 $\frac{5.6}{\square} = 5.6$

Ⓐ 0

Ⓑ 1

Ⓒ 5.6

Ⓓ 10

7 $1 \times 40{,}256 = \boxed{}$

Ⓐ 40,257

Ⓑ 40,256

Ⓒ 40,255

Ⓓ 1

8 $\frac{3\frac{1}{2}}{1} = \boxed{}$

Ⓐ 0   Ⓒ $3\frac{1}{2}$

Ⓑ 1   Ⓓ $4\frac{1}{2}$

9 Write the numbers that make the sentences true.

$\boxed{} \times 1 = 1{,}607$

$\frac{638}{\square} = 638$

$9{,}222 \times 0 = \boxed{}$

13 Mental Arithmetic to Add and Subtract

4.2.12: Use mental arithmetic to add or subtract numbers rounded to hundreds or thousands.

Mental arithmetic means doing arithmetic in your head. You do it without paper and pencil, and without a calculator.

Example 1

$300 + 600 = \boxed{}$

STRATEGY: **Follow these steps.**

    STEP 1: Take the same number of zeros away from each number.

                Remove 2 zeros from each number to get $3 + 6 = \boxed{}$.

    STEP 2: Add.

                $3 + 6 = 9$

    STEP 3: Place the 2 zeros back on the answer.

SOLUTION: $300 + 600 = 900$

Example 2

9,000 − 4,000 = ☐

STRATEGY: **Follow these steps.**

STEP 1:   Take the same number of zeros away from each number.

Remove 3 zeros from each number to get 9 − 4 = ☐.

STEP 2:   Subtract.

9 − 4 = 5

STEP 3:   Place the 3 zeros back on the answer.

SOLUTION: **9,000 − 4,000 = 5,000**

Sample Test Questions

1   200 + 400 = ☐

   Ⓐ 60

   Ⓑ 200

   Ⓒ 600

   Ⓓ 660

2   400 + 300 = ☐

   Ⓐ 70

   Ⓑ 100

   Ⓒ 700

   Ⓓ 7,000

3   800 − 200 = ☐

   Ⓐ 600

   Ⓑ 400

   Ⓒ 100

   Ⓓ 60

4   1,300 − 900 = ☐

   Ⓐ 2,700

   Ⓑ 500

   Ⓒ 400

   Ⓓ 200

5   4,000 + 6,000 = ☐

   Ⓐ 2,000

   Ⓑ 5,000

   Ⓒ 10,000

   Ⓓ 12,000

6   800 + 100 = ☐

   Ⓐ 700

   Ⓑ 800

   Ⓒ 900

   Ⓓ 1,000

7   700 − 400 = ☐

   Ⓐ 300

   Ⓑ 200

   Ⓒ 30

   Ⓓ 20

8   900 − 600 = ☐

   Ⓐ 1,500

   Ⓑ 1,200

   Ⓒ 700

   Ⓓ 300

9 $500 + 700 = \boxed{}$

Ⓐ 200

Ⓑ 1,000

Ⓒ 1,200

Ⓓ 1,500

10 $1,500 - 700 = \boxed{}$

Ⓐ 700

Ⓑ 800

Ⓒ 900

Ⓓ 1000

11 $13,000 - 8,000 = \boxed{}$

Ⓐ 5,000

Ⓑ 6,000

Ⓒ 7,000

Ⓓ 8,000

12 $600 + 800 = \boxed{}$

Ⓐ 14,000

Ⓑ 4,800

Ⓒ 1,400

Ⓓ 1,300

13   35,000 people attended Wednesday's baseball game. 4,000 more people attended Saturday's game than Wednesday's. How many people attended Saturday's baseball game?

_____

14 Adding and Subtracting Fractions

4.2.8: Add and subtract simple fractions with different denominators, using objects or pictures.

Same Denominators

Rule for adding two fractions with the same denominator:

Add the numerators, and place the sum over the denominator.

Rule for subtracting two fractions with the same denominator:

Subtract the numerators, place the difference over the denominator.

Example 1

$\frac{3}{7} + \frac{2}{7} = ?$

STRATEGY: **Use the rule for adding two fractions with the same denominator.**

STEP 1:   Add the numerators.

$3 + 2 = 5$

STEP 2:   Write the sum over the denominator.

$\frac{5}{7}$

SOLUTION: $\frac{3}{7} + \frac{2}{7} = \frac{5}{7}$

Different Denominators

To add or subtract two fractions with different denominators, your first have to find a common denominator.

Example 2

$\frac{1}{2} + \frac{1}{3} = ?$

STRATEGY: **Draw a diagram that will show a common denominator for $\frac{1}{2}$ and $\frac{1}{3}$.**

STEP 1: What is the least number of parts needed to show $\frac{1}{2}$ in a diagram?

To show $\frac{1}{2}$ you need 2 parts. Shade 1 of the parts.

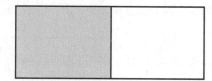

STEP 2: What is the least number of parts to show $\frac{1}{3}$ in a diagram?

To show $\frac{1}{3}$ you need 3 parts. Shade 1 of the parts.

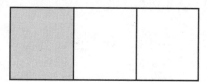

STEP 3: What is the least number of parts needed to show $\frac{1}{2}$ and $\frac{1}{3}$?

We need a number that can be divided into 2 parts (for $\frac{1}{2}$) and 3 parts (for $\frac{1}{3}$).

Think of a number that can be divided by 2 and 3.

The least number is 6.

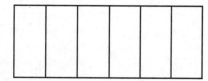

This diagram with 6 equal parts can be divided into halves (to show $\frac{1}{2}$) and thirds (to show $\frac{1}{3}$). This diagram with 6 equal parts shows sixths.

STEP 4: Shade the diagram to show $\frac{1}{2}$.

$$\frac{1}{2} = \frac{3}{6}$$

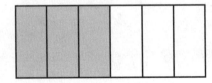

STEP 5: Shade another diagram to show $\frac{1}{3}$.

$$\frac{1}{3} = \frac{2}{6}$$

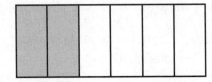

STEP 6: Show $\frac{1}{2} + \frac{1}{3}$ on another diagram.

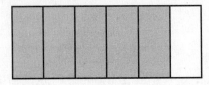

SOLUTION: $\frac{1}{2} + \frac{1}{3} \Rightarrow \frac{3}{6} + \frac{2}{6} = \frac{5}{6}$

Example 3

$\frac{1}{2} - \frac{1}{3} = ?$

STRATEGY: You can use the diagrams of Example 2 since the fractions ($\frac{1}{2}$ and $\frac{1}{3}$) are the same.

STEP 1: Follow the steps of Example 2 to Step 5.

STEP 2: To show $\frac{1}{2} - \frac{1}{3}$, first shade $\frac{1}{2}$, then shade $\frac{1}{3}$ in a different pattern over the shaded $\frac{1}{2}$, showing that $\frac{1}{3}$ is taken away.

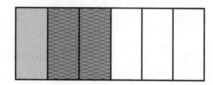

STEP 3: What is left after shading $\frac{1}{3}$ over the shaded $\frac{1}{2}$? $\frac{1}{6}$ of the rectangle is left.

SOLUTION: $\frac{1}{2} - \frac{1}{3} = \frac{1}{6}$

You can add or subtract two fractions with different denominators by

1. Making diagrams for each of the fractions.

2. Then finding the diagram that will work for both fractions.

Doing it this way is the same as finding the smallest number that both denominators divide. This number is the same as the number of equal parts of the diagram.

Sample Test Questions

1 $\frac{2}{5} + \frac{1}{5} = ?$

Ⓐ $\frac{3}{10}$

Ⓑ $\frac{1}{10}$

Ⓒ $\frac{1}{5}$

Ⓓ $\frac{3}{5}$

2 $\frac{2}{3} - \frac{1}{3} = ?$

Ⓐ $\frac{1}{3}$

Ⓑ $\frac{1}{6}$

Ⓒ $\frac{1}{9}$

Ⓓ $\frac{3}{6}$

3 $\frac{2}{3} - \frac{1}{6} = ?$

You can use this diagram.

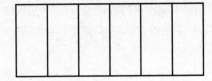

Ⓐ $\frac{5}{6}$

Ⓑ $\frac{1}{2}$

Ⓒ $\frac{1}{3}$

Ⓓ $\frac{1}{6}$

4 $\frac{4}{5} - \frac{1}{2} = ?$

Hint: Use a diagram divided into 10 equal parts.

Ⓐ $\frac{1}{10}$

Ⓑ $\frac{2}{5}$

Ⓒ $\frac{3}{10}$

Ⓓ $\frac{1}{5}$

5 $\frac{1}{4} + \frac{1}{2} = ?$

Ⓐ $\frac{5}{8}$

Ⓑ $\frac{3}{4}$

Ⓒ $\frac{2}{6}$

Ⓓ $\frac{1}{6}$

6 $\frac{3}{5} + \frac{1}{3} = ?$

Ⓐ $\frac{3}{5}$

Ⓑ $\frac{4}{5}$

Ⓒ $\frac{13}{15}$

Ⓓ $\frac{14}{15}$

7 $\frac{2}{7} + \frac{1}{2} = ?$

Ⓐ $\frac{3}{9}$

Ⓑ $\frac{1}{5}$

Ⓒ $\frac{11}{14}$

Ⓓ $\frac{13}{14}$

8 $\frac{3}{8} - \frac{1}{4} = ?$

Ⓐ $\frac{1}{8}$

Ⓑ $\frac{1}{4}$

Ⓒ $\frac{5}{8}$

Ⓓ $\frac{3}{4}$

9 After a party, there was $\frac{6}{8}$ of a pizza left. Joaquin ate $\frac{1}{2}$ of the leftover pizza. How much of a pizza was left after Joaquin was done? Draw a diagram that will help you solve this problem.

_____

15 Adding and Subtracting Decimals With Tenths and Hundredths

4.2.9: Add and subtract decimals (to hundredths), using objects or pictures.
4.2.10: Use a standard algorithm to add and subtract decimals (to hundredths).

The decimal 0.6 means the same as $\frac{6}{10}$.

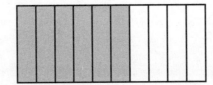

This diagram shows 0.6.

It means 6 of 10 equal parts.

Read 0.6 the same way that you read $\frac{6}{10}$.

You say "6 tenths."

You can use pictures to help you add and subtract decimals.

Example 1

What is the sum of 0.22 and 0.36?

STRATEGY: **Use a hundredths grid to find the sum.**

   STEP 1:   Shade 0.22 of the hundredths grid. (Shade 22 squares.)

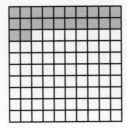

STEP 2: Shade 0.36 of the hundredths grid. (Shade another 36 squares.)

STEP 3: Count the number of squares shaded.

58 squares are shaded. This equals 0.58.

SOLUTION: **0.22 + 0.36 = 0.58**

Example 2

0.78 − 0.24 = ?

STRATEGY: **Use a hundredths grid to find the difference.**

STEP 1: Shade 0.78 of the hundredths grid. (Shade 78 squares.)

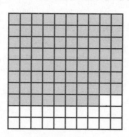

STEP 2: Cross out 24 of the shaded squares. This is the same as subtracting 0.24.

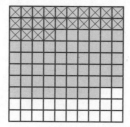

STEP 3: Count the shaded squares that have not been crossed out.

There are 54 shaded squares that have not been crossed out. This equals 0.54.

SOLUTION: **0.78 − 0.24 = 0.54**

How to Add Two Decimals

1. Write the numbers under each other.

2. Make sure the decimal points are lined up.

3. Add each place, starting at the right.

4. Place the decimal point in the sum, lined up under the other decimal points.

Example 3

Gil drove 5.32 miles on Monday and 6.15 miles on Tuesday. How far did he drive altogether?

STRATEGY: **Follow the steps above.**

$$
\begin{array}{r}
5.32 \\
+\ 6.15 \\
\hline
11.47
\end{array}
$$

SOLUTION: **Gil drove 11.47 miles altogether.**

Sample Test Questions

1 $3.6 + 2.9 = ?$

Ⓐ 5.5

Ⓑ 5.8

Ⓒ 6.4

Ⓓ 6.5

2 Marian spent 2.4 hours writing a report and 0.8 hour editing the report. How much time did it take her to complete the report?

Ⓐ 3.1 hours

Ⓑ 3.2 hours

Ⓒ 3.8 hours

Ⓓ 4.2 hours

3 What subtraction problem is shown by this picture?

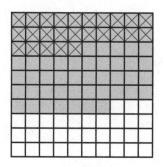

Ⓐ $0.57 - 0.25 = 0.32$

Ⓑ $0.67 - 0.25 = 0.42$

Ⓒ $0.67 - 0.35 = 0.32$

Ⓓ $0.57 - 0.35 = 0.22$

4 What addition problem is shown by this picture?

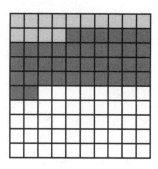

Ⓐ $0.14 + 0.38 = 0.52$

Ⓑ $0.24 + 0.38 = 0.62$

Ⓒ $0.18 + 0.34 = 0.52$

Ⓓ $0.28 + 0.34 = 0.62$

5 Niki walked 10.4 km and ran 4.6 km yesterday. How much farther did she walk than run?

Ⓐ 15 km

Ⓑ 6.8 km

Ⓒ 5.9 km

Ⓓ 5.8 km

6 Mario has two dogs. One weighs 3.4 pounds, and the other weighs 4.7 pounds. How much do the two dogs weigh altogether?

Ⓐ 8.3 pounds

Ⓑ 8.2 pounds

Ⓒ 8.1 pounds

Ⓓ 7.1 pounds

7 Felix brought two computers to a repair shop. The Acme computer weighed 16.5 pounds, and the Apex computer weighed 13.8 pounds. How much more did the Acme computer weigh than the Apex computer?

Ⓐ 3.7 pounds

Ⓑ 2.9 pounds

Ⓒ 2.7 pounds

Ⓓ 30.3 pounds

8 Marge's cat weighs 7.64 pounds more than Doris's cat. Doris's cat weighs 4.81 pounds. How much does Marge's cat weigh?

Ⓐ 2.85 pounds

Ⓑ 11.45 pounds

Ⓒ 11.95 pounds

Ⓓ 12.45 pounds

9 Use the hundredths grid below to show 0.39 + 0.52.

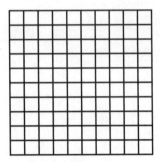

What is 0.39 + 0.52? _____

10 Melba slept 7.31 hours on Tuesday and 6.27 hours on Wednesday. How much longer did Melba sleep on Tuesday than on Wednesday? Show your work.

16 Using Estimation to Solve Problems

4.2.11: Know and use strategies for estimating results of any whole-number computations.
4.7.7: Know and use appropriate methods for estimating results of whole-number computations.

An estimate is an answer that is not exact. It should be close to the exact answer.

You can save time by estimating distances, amounts of money, weights, and other quantities in mathematical problems.

Example 1

Estimate. 8,151 + 3,902 = ☐

Ⓐ 5,000

Ⓑ 10,000

Ⓒ 11,000

Ⓓ 12,000

STRATEGY: **Since the answer choices are even thousands, round each number to the nearest 1,000.**

　　　　　　STEP 1: Round 8,151 to the nearest 1,000.

　　　　　　　　　　8,151 rounded to the nearest 1,000 is 8,000.

　　　　　　STEP 2: Round 3,902 to the nearest 1,000.

　　　　　　　　　　3,902 rounded to the nearest 1,000 is 4,000.

　　　　　　STEP 3: Add.

　　　　　　　　　　8,000 + 4,000 = 12,000

SOLUTION: **The best estimate is 12,000, Answer D.**

Example 2

Ricki earns $403.80 each week. About how much does she earn in a month?

STRATEGY: **Round numbers to make an estimate.**

> STEP 1:   Round $403.80 to the nearest 100 dollars.
>
> $403.80 rounded to the nearest hundred dollars is $400.
>
> STEP 2:   About how many weeks are there in a month?
>
> There are about 4 weeks in a month.
>
> STEP 3:   Multiply.
>
> $$\begin{array}{r} 400 \\ \times\ \ 4 \\ \hline 1{,}600 \end{array}$$

SOLUTION: **Ricki earns about $1,600 in a month. This is an estimate.**

Sample Test Questions

1 Round each amount to the nearest $10. Then estimate.

$456 − $203 = ☐

Ⓐ $200

Ⓑ $230

Ⓒ $260

Ⓓ $300

2 Tom saves $45.50 each month. Which is the best estimate of how much he will save at the end of six months?

Ⓐ $300

Ⓑ $500

Ⓒ $700

Ⓓ $900

For Questions 3-6, use the information in this table.

60 seconds = 1 minute
60 minutes = 1 hour
24 hours = 1 day
365 days = 1 year
52 weeks = 1 year

3 About how many minutes are there in 12 hours?

Ⓐ 60

Ⓑ 600

Ⓒ 6,000

Ⓓ 60,000

4 About how many hours are there in 8 days?

Ⓐ 50

Ⓑ 100

Ⓒ 150

Ⓓ 200

5 Vanessa's class uses the computer lab in her school for 28 minutes each day. What is a good estimate of how long her class uses the computer lab in 9 days?

Ⓐ 3 hours

Ⓑ 5 hours

Ⓒ 7 hours

Ⓓ 9 hours

6 About how many weeks are there in 9 years?

Ⓐ 45

Ⓑ 450

Ⓒ 600

Ⓓ 4,500

7 A new machine can print postage on envelopes at the rate of 72 envelopes per minute. Which is the best estimate of how many envelopes the machine can do in 9 minutes?

Ⓐ 400

Ⓑ 600

Ⓒ 800

Ⓓ 1,000

8 Estimate. $14,884 + 12,932 =$ ☐
(Round to the nearest 1,000.)

Ⓐ 2,000

Ⓑ 26,000

Ⓒ 27,000

Ⓓ 28,000

9 Estimate. $387 - 192 =$ ☐
(Round to the nearest 100.)

Ⓐ 100

Ⓑ 150

Ⓒ 200

Ⓓ 250

10 Chantel says that $3,469 + 5,213 = 7,682$. Without solving the problem, explain why you think Chantel's answer is wrong.

_____

_____

_____

_____

_____

Progress Check for
Lessons 7–16

1 Which multiplication fact is related to this division fact?

$$\frac{27}{9} = 3$$

Ⓐ $3 \times 3 = 9$

Ⓑ $27 \times 1 = 27$

Ⓒ $9 \times 3 = 27$

Ⓓ $6 \times 3 = 18$

2 There are 540 books in the history section of a library, and 250 books in the sports section. How many more books are in the history section than the sports section?

Ⓐ 280

Ⓑ 290

Ⓒ 320

Ⓓ 30

3 $57 \times 3 = ?$

Ⓐ 151

Ⓑ 158

Ⓒ 171

Ⓓ 178

4 $\frac{96}{4} = \boxed{}$

Ⓐ 32

Ⓑ 28

Ⓒ 24

Ⓓ 20

5 $65{,}097 + 22{,}458 = \boxed{}$

Ⓐ 87,655

Ⓑ 87,555

Ⓒ 87,545

Ⓓ 87,445

6 Each of the 20 students in Mr. Valducci's class donated 3 dollars to the school library. What is the total amount of money donated by Mr. Valducci's class?

Ⓐ 17 dollars

Ⓑ 23 dollars

Ⓒ 60 dollars

Ⓓ 100 dollars

7 Jan's mother paid for 7 meals for Jan and her friends at the museum. Each meal cost $8.95. Estimate how much the meals cost.

Ⓐ $50

Ⓑ $60

Ⓒ $70

Ⓓ $80

8 Divide 85 by 5.

Ⓐ 15

Ⓑ 16

Ⓒ 17

Ⓓ 18

9 Estimate. $78 \times 6 = ?$

Ⓐ 400

Ⓑ 480

Ⓒ 560

Ⓓ 640

10 Patty says she can type 52 words per minute. At that rate, about how many words can she type in 5 minutes?

Ⓐ 200

Ⓑ 250

Ⓒ 300

Ⓓ 350

11 $45.28 - 27.35 = \square$

Ⓐ 17.83

Ⓑ 17.93

Ⓒ 27.93

Ⓓ 72.63

12 $9 \times 7 = \square$

Ⓐ 54

Ⓑ 56

Ⓒ 62

Ⓓ 63

13 68 people can fit in 4 rows in the auditorium. How many people sit in each row if there are an equal number of people in each?

Ⓐ 72

Ⓑ 64

Ⓒ 17

Ⓓ 12

14 $8 \times \square = 48$

Ⓐ 4

Ⓑ 5

Ⓒ 6

Ⓓ 7

15 $4,623 + 2,870 = \square$

Ⓐ 7,493

Ⓑ 6,493

Ⓒ 7,393

Ⓓ 6,393

16 Students counted all the pencils in Mrs. Carmine's class. There were 88 pencils. Then the students placed the pencils in boxes that hold 8 each. How many boxes did they fill?

Ⓐ 16

Ⓑ 12

Ⓒ 11

Ⓓ 8

17 $234.8 \times \square = 234.8$

Ⓐ 0

Ⓑ 1

Ⓒ 10

Ⓓ 234.8

18 $2\frac{1}{2} \times \square = 0$

Ⓐ 100

Ⓑ 10

Ⓒ 1

Ⓓ 0

19 $\frac{738}{\square} = 738$

Ⓐ 0

Ⓑ 1

Ⓒ 100

Ⓓ 738

20 $\frac{1}{5} + \frac{1}{2} = \square$

Ⓐ $\frac{2}{7}$

Ⓑ $\frac{1}{10}$

Ⓒ $\frac{7}{10}$

Ⓓ $\frac{9}{10}$

21 $\frac{5}{8} - \frac{1}{2} = \square$

Ⓐ $\frac{1}{8}$

Ⓑ $\frac{1}{4}$

Ⓒ $\frac{4}{6}$

Ⓓ $\frac{3}{8}$

22 $5,000 + 9,000 = \square$

Ⓐ 4,000

Ⓑ 12,000

Ⓒ 14,000

Ⓓ 15,000

23 $56 \times 9 = \square$

Ⓐ 504

Ⓑ 454

Ⓒ 155

Ⓓ 65

24 $\frac{3}{4} - \frac{1}{8} = \square$

Ⓐ $\frac{4}{12}$

Ⓑ $\frac{6}{8}$

Ⓒ $\frac{5}{8}$

Ⓓ $\frac{1}{12}$

25 $16,000 - 9,000 = \square$

Ⓐ 25,000

Ⓑ 13,000

Ⓒ 8,000

Ⓓ 7,000

26 $23.47 + 18.29 = \square$

Ⓐ 5.18

Ⓑ 41.66

Ⓒ 41.76

Ⓓ 45.22

27 Kyria bakes 40 cookies. She wants to share the cookies equally among 5 people. How many cookies will each person get?

Ⓐ 45

Ⓑ 35

Ⓒ 15

Ⓓ 8

28 What subtraction problem is shown by this picture?

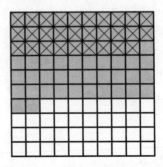

Ⓐ $0.62 - 0.19 = 0.43$

Ⓑ $0.62 - 0.29 = 0.33$

Ⓒ $0.52 - 0.19 - 0.33$

Ⓓ $0.52 - 0.29 = 0.23$

29 $12,000 - 4,000 = \square$

Ⓐ 16,000

Ⓑ 12,000

Ⓒ 10,000

Ⓓ 8,000

30 $49 \times 7 = \square$

Ⓐ 343

Ⓑ 243

Ⓒ 126

Ⓓ 56

Standard 2: Computation
Open-Ended Questions

1 List the different ways you could spend exactly $10.00 on these items. You can only buy one of each item.

T-shirt	$5.00
Toy car	$3.00
Stuffed giraffe	$2.50
Toy train	$7.00
Ball	$4.50
Puzzle	$2.00

_____

_____

_____

_____

2 Joanna rounded two 4-digit numbers to the nearest 100 and then added them. The answer was 3,500. Name two numbers that Joanna could have rounded. Explain your answer.

_____

_____

_____

_____

_____

3   Explain how you can find 8 × 9 by using a multiplication table. (See Lesson 8.)

_____

_____

_____

_____

_____

4   Find the quotient.

$6\overline{)96}$

Show your work.

Standard 3

Algebra and Functions

17 Numbers on a Number Line

4.3.8: Plot and label whole numbers on a number line up to 100. Estimate positions on the number line.

A number line can help you put numbers in order.

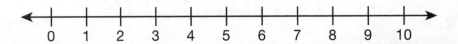

On the number line, 7 is to the right of 5. This tells you that 7 is greater than 5.

Here is a number line marked off by fives.

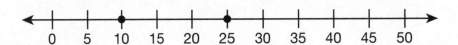

Notice that 10 is to the left of 25.

This tells you that 10 is less than 25.

Example 1

What number does point B stand for?

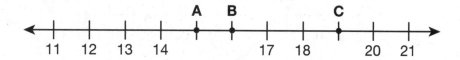

STRAGEGY: **First find the number that belongs at point A.**

The line is marked off in ones.

A is 1 interval to the right of 14, so A stands for 15.

B is 1 interval to the right of A. B is 1 more than A.

SOLUTION: **B stands for 16.**

Example 2

Which numbers do the points stand for?

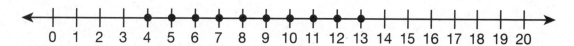

Ⓐ All whole numbers greater than 4 and less than 13

Ⓑ All whole numbers greater than 4 and less than 14

Ⓒ All whole numbers greater than 3 and less than 13

Ⓓ All whole numbers greater than 3 and less than 14

STRAGEGY: **Look at the points.**

The points show the numbers 4, 5, 6, 7, 8, 9, 10, 11, 12, and 13.

They are all greater than 3.

They are also less than 14.

SOLUTION: **So the answer is D.**

Example 3

Estimate the position of 77 on the number line.

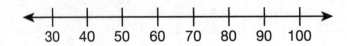

STRAGEGY: **Find the two numbers that 77 is between.**

77 is between 70 and 80 on the number line.

77 is closer to 80 than to 70.

SOLUTION:

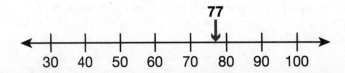

Sample Test Questions

1 Which letter shows the number 12?

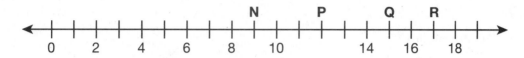

Ⓐ N Ⓒ Q

Ⓑ P Ⓓ R

2 What number belongs at S?

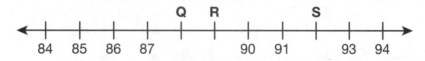

Ⓐ 88 Ⓒ 92

Ⓑ 89 Ⓓ 95

3 What number belongs at Z?

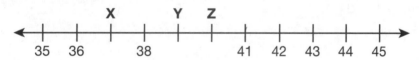

Ⓐ 37 Ⓒ 40

Ⓑ 39 Ⓓ 45

4 Which numbers do the dots stand for?

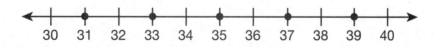

Ⓐ All even numbers greater than 30 and less than 40

Ⓑ All even numbers greater than 32 and less than 40

Ⓒ All odd numbers greater than 30 and less than 40

Ⓓ All even numbers greater than 30 and less than 42

5   Which numbers do the points stand for?

    Ⓐ   30, 35, 40, 45, 50

    Ⓑ   30, 40, 50, 60, 70

    Ⓒ   30, 40, 45, 50, 55

    Ⓓ   40, 50, 60

6   Which number line shows all whole numbers greater than 5 and less than 10?

7   On the number line below, estimate the position of 33.

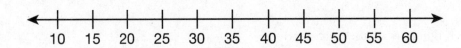

18 Completing Sentences

4.3.1: Use letters, boxes, or other symbols to represent any number in simple expressions, equations, or inequalities (i.e., demonstrate an understanding of and the use of the concept of a variable).

Sometimes you need to find a missing number or symbol in a mathematical sentence.

Example 1

What number completes this sentence?

$$\frac{\square}{3} = 2 \times 6$$

STRATEGY: **Think of what number replaces the $\square$ to make both sides equal.**

STEP 1: Compute the value of the right-hand side.

$2 \times 6 = 12$

The sentence now is $\frac{\square}{3} = 12$.

STEP 2: Read the sentence to yourself, replacing the $\square$ with the words "what number?"

$$\frac{\square}{3} = 12$$

"What number divided by 3 equals 12?"

STEP 3: Find the missing number.

36 divided by 3 equals 12.

SOLUTION: **The missing number is 36.**

Example 2

Which number completes the sentence?

0, 1, 2, 3

$$\square > \frac{4}{2}$$

(A) 0

(B) 1

(C) 2

(D) 3

STRATEGY: **Simplify the fraction, and then try each answer choice.**

STEP 1: Simplify $\frac{4}{2}$.

$$\frac{4 \div 2}{2 \div 2} = \frac{2}{1} = 2$$

STEP 2: Try each answer choice.

(A) $0 < 2$

(B) $1 < 2$

(C) $2 = 2$

(D) $3 > 2$

STEP 3: Since 3 is greater than 2, it completes the sentence.

SOLUTION: **The answer is D.**

Sample Test Questions

In Questions 1–8, find the number that makes each sentence true.

1 $\boxed{} \times 4 = 2 \times 8$

Ⓐ 4

Ⓑ 3

Ⓒ 2

Ⓓ 1

2 $27 - 3 = \dfrac{\boxed{}}{2}$

Ⓐ 2

Ⓑ 12

Ⓒ 24

Ⓓ 48

3 $23 + \boxed{} = 2 \times 18$

Ⓐ 18

Ⓑ 16

Ⓒ 13

Ⓓ 10

4 $\dfrac{25}{5} = 12 - \boxed{}$

Ⓐ 7

Ⓑ 6

Ⓒ 5

Ⓓ 12

5 $\boxed{} < \dfrac{6}{3}$

Ⓐ 1

Ⓑ 2

Ⓒ 3

Ⓓ 4

6 $0.75 < \boxed{}$

Ⓐ $\dfrac{60}{100}$

Ⓑ $\dfrac{70}{100}$

Ⓒ $\dfrac{75}{100}$

Ⓓ $\dfrac{80}{100}$

7 $\boxed{} = 1.5 + 1.5 + 0.5$

Ⓐ $1\frac{1}{2}$

Ⓑ $2\frac{1}{2}$

Ⓒ $3\frac{1}{2}$

Ⓓ $4\frac{1}{2}$

8 $0.4 > \boxed{}$

Ⓐ $\dfrac{3}{10}$

Ⓑ $\dfrac{4}{10}$

Ⓒ $\dfrac{5}{10}$

Ⓓ $\dfrac{6}{10}$

9 To make this sentence true, what number must ☐ stand for?

$$3 \times 13 = \boxed{} + 33$$

Ⓐ 39

Ⓑ 4

Ⓒ 5

Ⓓ 6

10 What number makes the sentence true?

$$\frac{200}{5} = \boxed{} \times 5$$

Ⓐ 10

Ⓑ 9

Ⓒ 8

Ⓓ 6

11 $\frac{1}{2}$ of $\boxed{} = 7 + 8$

Ⓐ 15

Ⓑ 20

Ⓒ 26

Ⓓ 30

12 Fill in the box with a number that completes the sentence.

$$10 \times \boxed{} = 35 + 5$$

13 Fill in the box with a number that completes the sentence.

$$\boxed{} > 2.5 + 1.5 + 0.5$$

19 Introduction to the Order of Operations

4.3.3: Understand that multiplication and division are performed before addition and subtraction in expressions without parentheses.

To find the value of expressions with more than one operation, you need to know which operation to do first.

Some expressions can be confusing. Take a look at this one:

$10 + 3 \times 23$

What do we do first: add 10 and 3, or multiply 3 and 23?

If we add 10 and 3 first and then multiply 23, we get 299 as an answer.

$10 + 3 = 13$
$13 \times 23 = 299$

If we multiply 3 and 23 and then add 10, we get 79 as an answer.

$3 \times 23 = 69$
$69 + 10 = 79$

How do we know which answer is right?

To clarify which operation goes first, use a rule called Order of Operations.

Order of Operations
Multiply and divide before you add or subtract.

Example 1

$$10 + 3 \times 23 = ?$$

STRATEGY: **Use the order of operations.**

> **STEP 1:**   Multiply first. $3 \times 23 = 69$
>
> **STEP 2:**   Then add 10. $69 + 10 = 79$

SOLUTION: $10 + 3 \times 23 = 79$

Example 2

$$\frac{40}{8} - 2 = ?$$

STRATEGY: **Use the order of operations.**

> **STEP 1:**   Divide first. $\frac{40}{8} = 5$
>
> **STEP 2:**   Then subtract 2. $5 - 2 = 3$

SOLUTION: $\frac{40}{8} - 2 = 3$

Example 3

Michael went to the store with 80 cents. He bought 3 pencils that cost 10 cents each. Which expression shows how much change he received?

   Ⓐ $80 + 3 \times 10$ Ⓒ $80 - 3 + 10$

   Ⓑ $80 - 3 \times 10$ Ⓓ $80 + 3 + 10$

STRATEGY: **Subtract how much money he spent from how much money he started with.**

> **STEP 1:**   Write the multiplication part of the expression first. This shows how much money he spent.
>
> 3 pencils $\times$ 10 cents each
>
> 3×10
>
> **STEP 2:**   Then subtract from the amount of money he started with.
>
> $80 - 3 \times 10$

SOLUTION: **The answer is B.**

Sample Test Questions

For Questions 1–5, use the order of operations.

1 $30 - 10 \times 2 = ?$

    Ⓐ 40

    Ⓑ 30

    Ⓒ 20

    Ⓓ 10

2 $88 + \frac{12}{4} = ?$

    Ⓐ 91

    Ⓑ 85

    Ⓒ 50

    Ⓓ 25

3 $\frac{200}{25} - 5 = ?$

    Ⓐ 20

    Ⓑ 10

    Ⓒ 4

    Ⓓ 3

4 $76 \times 4 - 1 = ?$

    Ⓐ 305

    Ⓑ 304

    Ⓒ 303

    Ⓓ 228

5 $\frac{1000}{20} + \frac{30}{6} = ?$

    Ⓐ 4

    Ⓑ 40

    Ⓒ 55

    Ⓓ 56

6   Gary went shopping with $20. He bought 7 pens at $1.50 each. Which expression shows how much change he got?

    Ⓐ $20 - 7 + 1.50$

    Ⓑ $20 + 7 \times 1.50$

    Ⓒ $20 - 7 \times 1.50$

    Ⓓ $20 \times 7 \times 1.50$

7   Jessica started the day with $10. She baby-sat for a neighbor and received $7 per hour. Which expression shows how much money she had at the end of the day after baby-sitting for $5\frac{1}{2}$ hours?

    Ⓐ $7 \times 5\frac{1}{2}$

    Ⓑ $10 - 7 \times 5\frac{1}{2}$

    Ⓒ $10 + 7 \times 5\frac{1}{2}$

    Ⓓ $10 \times 5\frac{1}{2} + 7$

8 The paper company's delivery truck carried 30 packages. Fourteen packages weighed 20 pounds each and the remainder weighed 15 pounds each. Which expression shows the total weight of the packages?

Ⓐ $14 \times 20 + 16 \times 15$

Ⓑ $14 \times 20 + 30 \times 15$

Ⓒ $15 + 20 + 16 + 15$

Ⓓ $15 \times 20 \times 16 \times 15$

9 Caroline had $20. She walked her neighbor's dog for $8 per hour. Write an expression that shows how much money she had after walking the dog for 3 hours.

_____

20 Finding Values for Variables

4.3.4: Understand that an equation such as $y = 3x + 5$ is a rule for finding a second number when a first number is given.

Variables are letters such as x and y that stand for numbers. You will see them in number sentences such as $3x - 7 = 13$ or $y - 10 = 2$.

The sentence $y = 3x + 5$ has two variables in the same sentence. It shows the relationship between the numbers x and y.

$3x$ means 3 times x.

$3x + 5$ means add $3x$ and 5.

$y = 3x + 5$ means that y has the same value as $3x + 5$.

Example 1

For the sentence $y = 4x - 1$, find the value of y when $x = 5$.

STRATEGY: **Substitute the *x*-value and compute.**

STEP 1: Substitute the x-value of 5 in the sentence.

Remember that $4x$ means 4 times x.

$y = 4 \times 5 - 1$

STEP 2: Compute the answer.

$y = 4 \times 5 - 1 = 20 - 1 = 19$

SOLUTION: **For the sentence $y = 4x - 1$, the y-value is 19 when the x-value is 5.**

Example 2

For the sentence $y = 5x + 4$, find the y-values for x values of 0, 1, 2, 3, and 4.

STRATEGY: **Make a table of values.**

STEP 1: Set up a table for x- and y-values.

This is one way to set up a table.

x					
y					

STEP 2: Put the x-values in the table.

x	0	1	2	3	4
y					

STEP 3: Substitute each x-value into the equation. Then compute the y-values.

For $x = 0$, $y = 5x + 4 = 5 \times 0 + 4 = 0 + 4 = 4$

For $x = 1$, $y = 5x + 4 = 5 \times 1 + 4 = 5 + 4 = 9$

For $x = 2$, $y = 5x + 4 = 5 \times 2 + 4 = 10 + 4 = 14$

For $x = 3$, $y = 5x + 4 = 5 \times 3 + 4 = 15 + 4 = 19$

For $x = 4$, $y = 5x + 4 = 5 \times 4 + 4 = 20 + 4 = 24$

STEP 4: In the table, fill in the y-values.

Make sure to put each y-value with its x-value.

x	0	1	2	3	4
y	4	9	14	19	24

SOLUTION: **The y-values are 4, 9, 14, 19, and 24.**

Sample Test Questions

1 For the sentence $y = 4x$, what is the y-value when $x = 2$?

Ⓐ 2

Ⓑ 4

Ⓒ 6

Ⓓ 8

2 For the sentence $y = x + 20$, what is the y-value when $x = 11$?

Ⓐ 11

Ⓑ 21

Ⓒ 31

Ⓓ 41

3 For the sentence $y = 3x - 2$, what is the value of y when $x = 100$?

Ⓐ 300

Ⓑ 298

Ⓒ 296

Ⓓ 100

4 For the sentence $y = 2x$, what are the missing y-values in this table?

x	2	4	6
y			

Ⓐ 4, 5, 6

Ⓑ 4, 8, 12

Ⓒ 2, 8, 12

Ⓓ 4, 6, 8

5 For the sentence $y = 5x - 2$, what are the missing y-values in this table?

x	1	2	3	4
y				

Ⓐ 3, 8, 13, 18

Ⓑ 3, 6, 9, 12

Ⓒ 4, 8, 16, 18

Ⓓ 5, 10, 15, 20

6 For the sentence $y = 4x + 3$, complete the table for the missing y-values.

x	1	2	3	4
y				

7 For the sentence $y = 6x - 4$, complete the table for the missing y-values.

x	2	4	6	8
y				

21 Multiplication as Repeated Addition and Division as Repeated Subtraction

4.2.2: Represent as multiplication any situation involving repeated addition.

4.3.6: Recognize and apply the relationships between addition and multiplication, between subtraction and division, and the inverse relationship between multiplication and division to solve problems.

$$12 + 12 + 12 + 12 + 12 = 60$$

The number sentence shows repeated addition: 12 is added 5 times. Another way to represent this problem is as a multiplication sentence.

$$5 \times 12 = 60$$

Multiplication is repeated addition.

Example 1

Find another way of writing $4 + 4 + 4 + 4 + 4 + 4 + 4$.

STRATEGY: **Multiplication is repeated addition.**

STEP 1: Count the number of times 4 is added.

4 is added 7 times.

STEP 2: Because you add the same number repeatedly, you can change the expression to a multiplication expression.

7×4

SOLUTION: **Another way of writing $4 + 4 + 4 + 4 + 4 + 4 + 4$ is 7×4.**

Just as multiplication is repeated addition, division is repeated subtraction.

If you have 20 apples, and you want to put them in bags with 5 apples each, how many bags will you need?

Here is one way to solve the problem. Start by putting 5 apples in a bag. Continue subtracting 5 apples until there are no apples left. Then count the number of times you subtracted 5.

$$20 - 5 - 5 - 5 - 5 = 0$$

You need 4 bags.

Another way to solve this problem is to use division.

$$20 \div 5 = 4$$

You can think of division as repeated subtraction.

Example 2

Find another way of writing $36 - 6 - 6 - 6 - 6 - 6 - 6$.

STRATEGY: **Think of division as repeated subtraction.**

        STEP 1:   Count the number of times you subtract 6 from 36 to get 0.

                       6 is subtracted 6 times.

        STEP 2:   Because you subtract the same number over and over, change the subtraction expression to a division expression.

SOLUTION: **36 ÷ 6**

Example 3

Use $5 \times 15 = 75$ to find $75 \div 5 = ?$

STRATEGY: **Use the inverse relationship between multiplication and division.**

        STEP 1:   Change the multiplication sentence to related division sentences. (Find the division members of the fact family.)

                       Remember, multiplication and division are opposites of each other.

                       The opposites of $5 \times 15 = 75$ are:

                       $75 \div 5 = 15$ and $75 \div 15 = 5$

        STEP 2:   Choose the sentence of Step 1 that works for this example.

SOLUTION: **75 ÷ 5 = 15**

Sample Test Questions

1 What is another way to write 11 + 11 + 11 + 11 + 11 + 11 + 11 + 11 + 11?

Ⓐ 9 + 11

Ⓑ 11 ÷ 9

Ⓒ 9 × 11

Ⓓ 11 × 11

2 What is another way to write 48 − 6 − 6 − 6 − 6 − 6 − 6 − 6 − 6?

Ⓐ 48 − 6

Ⓑ 48 ÷ 6

Ⓒ 48 + 6

Ⓓ 48 ÷ 7

3 What is another way to write 9 + 9 + 9 + 9?

Ⓐ 1 × 9

Ⓑ 2 × 9

Ⓒ 3 × 9

Ⓓ 4 × 9

4 What is another way to write 5 × 6?

Ⓐ 6 + 6 + 6

Ⓑ 6 + 6 + 6 + 6

Ⓒ 6 + 6 + 6 + 6 + 6

Ⓓ 6 + 6 + 6 + 6 + 6 + 6

5 What division expression is shown by this expression?

72 − 9 − 9 − 9 − 9 − 9 − 9 − 9 − 9

Ⓐ 72 ÷ 9

Ⓑ 72 ÷ 0

Ⓒ 72 ÷ 7

Ⓓ 72 ÷ 6

6 Dana ran 2 miles each day for 8 days in a row. She wanted to figure out how many miles she ran altogether. She calculated 2 + 2 + 2 + 2 + 2 + 2 + 2 + 2. What is another way to figure out how many miles Dana ran?

Ⓐ 5 × 2

Ⓑ 6 × 2

Ⓒ 7 × 2

Ⓓ 8 × 2

7 Which equation is the inverse of the division sentence?

203 ÷ 7 = 29

Ⓐ 29 × 203 = 7

Ⓑ 203 ÷ 29 = 7

Ⓒ 29 × 7 = 203

Ⓓ 203 × 7 = 29

8 Janna picked 7 apples each day for 9 days. Show how you would use repeated addition to find how many apples she picked altogether.

_____

_____

Show how you could use multiplication to find how many apples she picked altogether.

_____

_____

9 Write two multiplication sentences that belong in the same fact family as $126 \div 18 = 7$.

_____

_____

22 Patterns Using Multiplication and Division

4.3.5: Continue number patterns using multiplication and division.

Some patterns are based on multiplying or dividing. This means that the next number of a pattern is the result of multiplying or dividing the number before by a certain number.

Example 1

What is the next number of this sequence?

3, 9, 27, 81, ___

STRATEGY: **Find the rule for finding the next number.**

STEP 1: How many times greater is the second number than the first number?

9 is 3 times 3.

STEP 2: How many times greater is the third number than the second number?

27 is 3 times 9.

STEP 3: How many times greater is the fourth number than the third number?

81 is 3 times 27.

STEP 4: What is the rule for the pattern?

The rule is "multiply by 3."

STEP 5: Use the rule to find the fifth number.

$81 \times 3 = 243$

SOLUTION: **The missing number is 243.**

Example 2

What is the next number in the sequence?

800, 400, 200, 100, ____

STRATEGY: **Find the rule for finding the next number.**

STEP 1: Compare the second number to the first number.
400 is 800 divided by 2.

STEP 2: Compare the third number to the second number.
200 is 400 divided by 2.

STEP 3: Compare the fourth number to the third number.
100 is 200 divided by 2.

STEP 4: What is the rule for the pattern?
The rule is "divide by 2."

STEP 5: Use the rule to find the fifth number.
$\frac{100}{2} = 50$

SOLUTION: **The next number is 50.**

Sample Test Questions

For questions 1–7, find the missing number in the sequence.

1   1, 4, 16, 64, ____

   Ⓐ 250

   Ⓑ 252

   Ⓒ 256

   Ⓓ 258

2   800, 400, 200, 100, 50, ____

   Ⓐ 20

   Ⓑ 25

   Ⓒ 30

   Ⓓ 35

3   2, 6, 18, 54, ____

   Ⓐ 150

   Ⓑ 160

   Ⓒ 162

   Ⓓ 172

4   891, 297, 99, 33, ____

   Ⓐ 20

   Ⓑ 11

   Ⓒ 8

   Ⓓ 5

5   3, 6, 12, 24, ____

   Ⓐ 40

   Ⓑ 42

   Ⓒ 46

   Ⓓ 48

6   360, 120, 90, 30, ____

   Ⓐ 10

   Ⓑ 20

   Ⓒ 30

   Ⓓ 40

7   4, 12, 36, ____

   Ⓐ 106

   Ⓑ 108

   Ⓒ 110

   Ⓓ 112

For questions 8–10, find the missing number in the sequence and the rule for the pattern.

8 240, 120, 60, 30, ____

  Ⓐ 10, divide by 2

  Ⓑ 10, divide by 3

  Ⓒ 15, divide by 2

  Ⓓ 20, divide by 3

9 7, 14, 28, 56, ____

  Ⓐ 100, multiply by 2

  Ⓑ 110, multiply by 4

  Ⓒ 110, multiply by 2

  Ⓓ 112, multiply by 2

10 343, 49, ____, 1

  Ⓐ 3, divide by 3

  Ⓑ 7, divide by 7

  Ⓒ 9, divide by 9

  Ⓓ 11, divide by 11

11 Fill in the next two numbers for the sequence below.

  9, 18, 36, ____, ____

  Write the rule on the line below.

  _____

12 Fill in the missing numbers for the sequence below.

  ____, ____, 9, 3, 1

  Write the rule on the line below.

  _____

23 Writing Number Sentences for Multiplication and Division

4.3.1: Use letters, boxes, or other symbols to represent any number in simple expressions, equations, or inequalities (i.e., demonstrate an understanding of and the use of the concept of a variable).
4.3.7: Relate problem situations to number sentences involving multiplication and division.

You can write number sentences to help you solve word problems with multiplication and division.

Example 1

Janet bought 7 cookbooks. They were each $9. Write a number sentence to show how to find out how much money she spent in all.

STRATEGY: **Figure out if the problem involves multiplication or division.**

STEP 1: You could add $9 seven times—or multiply.

STEP 2: Write a multiplication sentence that will help you find the answer.

SOLUTION: $7 \times 9 = \boxed{}$

Example 2

Edward has 80 cookies that he would like to share equally among the 20 members of his class. Which number sentence shows how many cookies each person will get?

(A) $80 \div 20 = \boxed{}$

(B) $80 \times 20 = \boxed{}$

(C) $80 \div 30 = \boxed{}$

(D) $80 \times 30 = \boxed{}$

STRATEGY: **Determine which number sentence will help you solve the problem.**

STEP 1:   Does the problem involve multiplication or division?

Edward wants to share his 80 cookies equally among 20 people, so use division.

STEP 2:   Write a division sentence that will help you find the answer.

$80 \div 20 = \boxed{}$

SOLUTION: **The answer is A.**

Sample Test Questions

1   Kristin read 15 pages in her book each day. She read her book for 7 days. Which number sentence shows how to figure out how many pages she read in all?

(A) $7 + 15 = \boxed{}$

(B) $15 - 7 = \boxed{}$

(C) $7 \times 15 = \boxed{}$

(D) $15 \div 7 = \boxed{}$

2   Meredith bought 55 pencils. She wants to give an equal number of pencils to each of her 11 friends. Which number sentence shows how to find how many pencils she will give to each friend?

(A) $55 \times 11 = \boxed{}$

(B) $55 \times 12 = \boxed{}$

(C) $55 \div 11 = \boxed{}$

(D) $55 \div 12 = \boxed{}$

3   Kelly runs 4 miles each day. Which number sentence shows how to find how many miles she runs in 9 days?

(A) $9 \times 4 = \boxed{}$

(B) $10 \times 4 = \boxed{}$

(C) $9 \div 4 = \boxed{}$

(D) $9 \div 7 = \boxed{}$

4   Jennifer buys 72 balloons. She wants to share the balloons equally among her 8 friends. Which number sentence shows how to find how many balloons each friend will get?

(A) $72 \times 8 = \boxed{}$

(B) $72 \times 2 = \boxed{}$

(C) $72 \div 2 = \boxed{}$

(D) $72 \div 8 = \boxed{}$

5   Maggie makes $9 an hour delivering newspapers. Which number sentence shows how much money she makes in 14 hours?

(A) $14 \div 9 = \boxed{}$

(B) $14 \div 7 = \boxed{}$

(C) $14 \times 9 = \boxed{}$

(D) $14 \times 7 = \boxed{}$

6   Ben has 48 baseball cards. He wants to share his baseball cards equally among 3 friends. Which number sentence shows how many baseball cards each friend will get?

(A) $48 \times 3 = \boxed{}$

(B) $48 \div 3 = \boxed{}$

(C) $48 \times 5 = \boxed{}$

(D) $48 \div 5 = \boxed{}$

7 Caroline has 96 stickers she wants to share equally among her 6 friends. Write a number sentence that shows how many stickers each friend will get.

_____

8 Write a problem that you can describe with the sentence $10 \times 8 = \boxed{}$.

_____

_____

_____

_____

_____

_____

Progress Check for Lessons 17–23

1 What number makes the sentence true?

$\boxed{} > 0.74$

(A) $\frac{1}{4}$

(B) $\frac{2}{4}$

(C) $\frac{3}{4}$

(D) $\frac{3}{6}$

2 For $y = 6x$, find the value of y when $x = 13$.

(A) 81

(B) 78

(C) 19

(D) 7

3 Which letter shows the number 35?

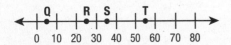

(A) Q

(B) R

(C) S

(D) T

4 $15 \times 3 - 6 = \boxed{}$

(A) 40

(B) 39

(C) 38

(D) 37

5 Find the number that makes the sentence true.

$6 \times \boxed{} = 30 - 12$

(A) 20

(B) 18

(C) 6

(D) 3

6 Jessica went to a store with $37 and bought 2 books for $4 each. Which expression shows how much money she had left?

(A) $37 + 2 + 4$

(B) $37 \div 2 - 4$

(C) $37 \times 2 - 4$

(D) $37 - 2 \times 4$

7 Find the missing number in the sequence.

4, 8, 16, 32, 64, ____

Ⓐ 122

Ⓑ 124

Ⓒ 126

Ⓓ 128

8 Find the number that makes the sentence true.

$$\frac{\square}{8} = \frac{14}{7}$$

Ⓐ 20

Ⓑ 18

Ⓒ 16

Ⓓ 13

9 Which point shows 65 on this number line?

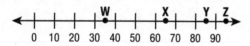

Ⓐ W

Ⓑ X

Ⓒ Y

Ⓓ Z

10 For $y = 7x - 5$, find the value of y when $x = 6$.

Ⓐ 40

Ⓑ 39

Ⓒ 38

Ⓓ 37

11 What is another way to write $5 + 5 + 5 + 5 = \square$?

Ⓐ $4 \times 3 = \square$

Ⓑ $4 \times 4 = \square$

Ⓒ $4 \times 5 = \square$

Ⓓ $4 \div 5 = \square$

12 Collin bought 9 packs of baseball cards. Each pack costs $2. Which number sentence shows how much money Collin spent?

Ⓐ $9 \times 2 = \square$

Ⓑ $9 \div 2 = \square$

Ⓒ $9 \times 9 = \square$

Ⓓ $9 \div 9 = \square$

13 For the sentence, $y = 2x + 2$, what are the missing y-values in this table?

x	1	2	3	4
y				

Ⓐ 4, 5, 6, 7

Ⓑ 4, 6, 8, 10

Ⓒ 2, 4, 6, 8

Ⓓ 4, 8, 12, 16

14 Find the number that makes the sentence true.

$$6 + \boxed{} = 48 \div 3$$

Ⓐ 10

Ⓑ 12

Ⓒ 14

Ⓓ 16

15 $4 + \frac{28}{4} = \boxed{}$

Ⓐ 9

Ⓑ 10

Ⓒ 11

Ⓓ 12

16 What number does point Y stand for?

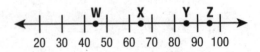

Ⓐ 85

Ⓑ 80

Ⓒ 75

Ⓓ 70

17 Find the missing number in the sequence.

$$81, 27, \underline{\hphantom{000}}, 3, 1$$

Ⓐ 9

Ⓑ 11

Ⓒ 13

Ⓓ 15

18 What expression is related to $42 - 7 - 7 - 7 - 7 - 7 - 7$?

Ⓐ $42 \div 7$

Ⓑ $42 \div 0$

Ⓒ 42×7

Ⓓ 42×0

19 Find the missing number in the sequence and the rule for finding the next number.

$$256, 64, 16, 4, \underline{\hspace{1cm}}$$

Ⓐ 0; multiply by 2

Ⓑ 1; multiply by 2

Ⓒ 1; divide by 4

Ⓓ 0; divide by 4

20 What is another way to write $27 + 27 + 27 + 27 + 27 + 27 = \boxed{}$?

Ⓐ $27 \times 27 = \boxed{}$

Ⓑ $27 \div 27 = \boxed{}$

Ⓒ $27 \div 6 = \boxed{}$

Ⓓ $6 \times 27 = \boxed{}$

21 Greta has 81 crayons. She wants to share her crayons equally among 9 of her friends. Which number sentence shows how many crayons each friend will get?

Ⓐ $81 \times 9 = \boxed{}$

Ⓑ $81 \div 9 = \boxed{}$

Ⓒ $81 \times 81 = \boxed{}$

Ⓓ $81 \div 81 = \boxed{}$

22 Christina makes $7 an hour mowing her neighbor's lawn. Which number sentence shows how much money she makes after 13 hours?

Ⓐ $13 \div 7 = \boxed{}$

Ⓑ $13 \div 13 = \boxed{}$

Ⓒ $13 \times 7 = \boxed{}$

Ⓓ $13 \times 13 = \boxed{}$

23 Fill in the boxes with the number that completes the sentence.

Ⓐ $24 \times 2 = \boxed{} + 8$

Ⓑ $55 \div 11 = 11 - \boxed{}$

Ⓒ $\boxed{} \times 7 = 60 + 3$

Ⓓ $55 \div \boxed{} = 20 \div 4$

Standard 3: Algebra and Functions
Open-Ended Questions

1   Annie had $40. She watered her neighbor's plants for $5 an hour. Write a number sentence that shows how much money she had after 8 hours of watering plants.

_____

2   For the sentence $y = 9x - 6$, complete the table for the missing y-values.

x	3	5	7	9
y				

3   Find the missing numbers in the sequence.

4, 12, 36, _____, _____

Write the rule.

_____

4   Write two division sentences that are related to $13 \times 4 = 52$.

_____

_____

Standard

4

Geometry

24 Parallel and Perpendicular Lines

4.4.2: Identify, describe, and draw parallel, perpendicular, and oblique lines using appropriate mathematical tools and technology.

Parallel Lines

Lines that are always the same distance apart are parallel.

Example 1

Which line is parallel to line *q*?

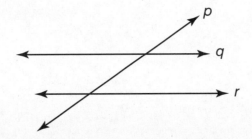

STRATEGY: **Remember that parallel lines are always the same distance apart.**

Look for lines that are the same distance apart.

Line *r* is always the same distance from line *q*.

SOLUTION: **Line *r* is parallel to line *q*.**

In Example 1, line *p* intersects (or crosses) lines *q* and *r*.

Perpendicular Lines

Lines that intersect at right angles are called perpendicular lines. A right angle forms a square corner.

Example 2

Which line is perpendicular to line *a*?

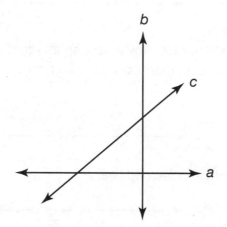

STRATEGY: **Remember that perpendicular lines intersect at right angles, and that right angles form square corners.**

Find the square corners.

Line *b* makes 4 square corners where it crosses line *a*.

SOLUTION: **Line *b* is perpendicular to line *a*.**

Example 3

Draw two lines that are parallel.

STRATEGY: **Use a ruler.**

      STEP 1:   Use a ruler to draw a line.

      STEP 2:   Measure to draw a second line that is always the same distance apart from your first line.

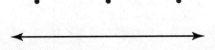

      STEP 3:   Draw the second line.

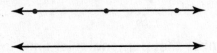

SOLUTION: **The two lines are parallel.**

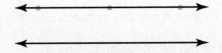

Sample Test Questions

1 Which two lines are parallel?

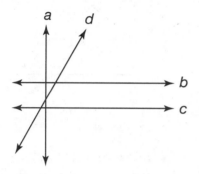

- Ⓐ *a* and *b*
- Ⓑ *b* and *c*
- Ⓒ *a* and *d*
- Ⓓ *a* and *c*

2 Which two lines are perpendicular?

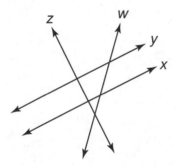

- Ⓐ *w* and *y*
- Ⓑ *y* and *x*
- Ⓒ *w* and *z*
- Ⓓ *x* and *z*

3 Which statement is correct?

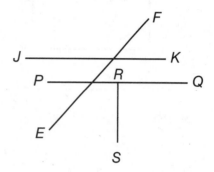

- Ⓐ $\overline{PQ}$ is parallel to $\overline{RS}$.
- Ⓑ $\overline{PQ}$ is perpendicular to $\overline{RS}$.
- Ⓒ $\overline{PQ}$ is perpendicular to $\overline{JK}$.
- Ⓓ $\overline{EF}$ is parallel to $\overline{RS}$.

4 Which edge is parallel to edge *ZW*?

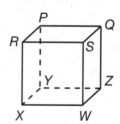

- Ⓐ $\overline{PQ}$
- Ⓑ $\overline{SW}$
- Ⓒ $\overline{XY}$
- Ⓓ $\overline{YZ}$

5 Which segment is perpendicular to $\overline{MN}$?

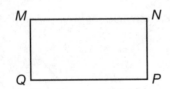

Ⓐ $\overline{NP}$

Ⓑ $\overline{PQ}$

Ⓒ $\overline{QN}$

Ⓓ $\overline{MP}$

6 Which edge is parallel to edge PQ?

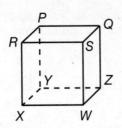

Ⓐ $\overline{QZ}$

Ⓑ $\overline{SW}$

Ⓒ $\overline{YZ}$

Ⓓ $\overline{XY}$

7 Which statement is correct?

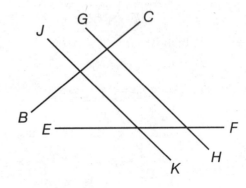

Ⓐ $\overline{BC}$ is parallel to $\overline{EF}$.

Ⓑ $\overline{BC}$ intersects $\overline{GH}$.

Ⓒ $\overline{BC}$ is parallel to $\overline{JK}$.

Ⓓ $\overline{JK}$ is parallel to $\overline{EF}$.

8 Draw two lines that are parallel. Draw a third line that is perpendicular to the parallel lines.

25 Angles

4.4.1: Identify, describe, and draw rays, right angles, acute angles, obtuse angles, and straight angles using appropriate mathematical tools and technology.

Parts of Angles

An angle is formed by two rays that meet at a common point.

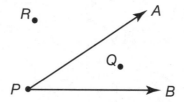

P is called the vertex of angle APB. When an angle is named, the vertex is always the middle letter of the name.

Rays PA and PB are the sides of the angle.

Point Q is in the interior of the angle and Point R is in the exterior of the angle.

Types of Angles

You need to know the four different types of angles.

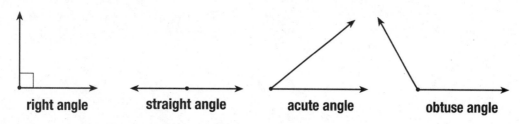

right angle—an angle that forms a square corner

straight angle—an angle that forms a straight line

acute angle—an angle whose measure is less than that of a right angle

obtuse angle—an angle whose measure is greater than that of a right angle

131

Example

What type of angle is angle Z?

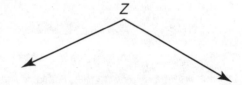

STRATEGY: **Is the measure of angle Z less than or greater than that of a right angle?**

The measure of angle Z is greater than that of a right angle.

SOLUTION: **Angle Z is an obtuse angle.**

132

Sample Test Questions

1 Which letter represents the vertex of the angle?

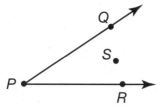

- Ⓐ *P*
- Ⓑ *Q*
- Ⓒ *R*
- Ⓓ *S*

2 Which angle is an obtuse angle?

Ⓐ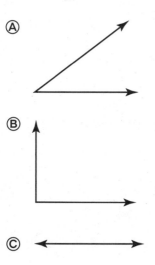

Ⓑ

Ⓒ

Ⓓ

3 Connect points *P*, *Q*, and *R* to form angle *PQR*. Then choose the correct statement below.

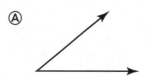

- Ⓐ This is an acute angle.
- Ⓑ This is a right angle.
- Ⓒ This is an obtuse angle.
- Ⓓ The measure of the angle is equal to 120°.

4 Which of the following is not an acute angle?

Ⓐ

Ⓑ

Ⓒ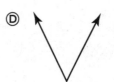

Ⓓ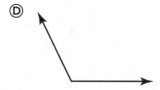

5   Where is point *F* located?

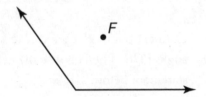

 Ⓐ in the interior of the angle

 Ⓑ in the exterior of the angle

 Ⓒ on the rays of the angle

 Ⓓ at the vertex of the angle

6   Draw two rays that form an obtuse angle.

7   Draw two rays that form a right angle.

26 | Two-Dimensional Figures

4.4.3: Identify, describe, and draw parallelograms, rhombuses, and trapezoids, using appropriate mathematical tools and technology.

Here are some geometric figures you should know.

triangle   A closed figure with three sides and three angles

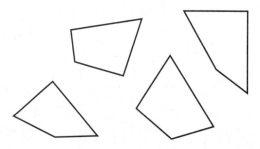

quadrilateral   A closed figure with four sides and four angles

parallelogram   A quadrilateral with opposite sides parallel

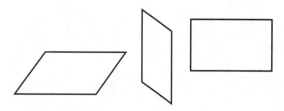

rectangle A parallelogram with four square corners (four right angles)

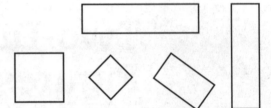

square A rectangle with all sides equal in length

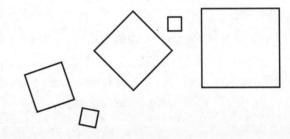

rhombus A parallelogram with all sides equal in length

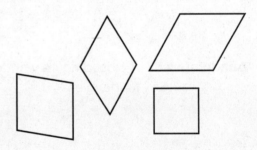

trapezoid A quadrilateral with only two sides parallel

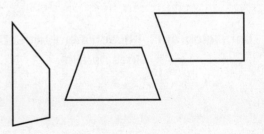

Sample Test Questions

1 What is the name of a quadrilateral with four square corners?

Ⓐ trapezoid

Ⓑ rectangle

Ⓒ congruent

Ⓓ triangle

2 What is the name of the figure?

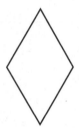

Ⓐ trapezoid

Ⓑ square

Ⓒ rhombus

Ⓓ rectangle

3 Which statement is not true?

Ⓐ A rhombus always has 4 square corners.

Ⓑ A parallelogram has 2 pairs of parallel sides.

Ⓒ A quadrilateral has 4 angles.

Ⓓ A rectangle has 4 right angles.

4 Which of the following is not a parallelogram?

Ⓐ

Ⓑ

Ⓒ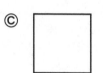

Ⓓ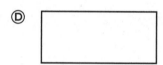

5 What is the name of the figure?

Ⓐ rectangle

Ⓑ rhombus

Ⓒ trapezoid

Ⓓ congruent

6 What is the name of a quadrilateral with all sides equal in length?

Ⓐ parallelogram

Ⓑ rhombus

Ⓒ trapezoid

Ⓓ hexagon

7 What is the name of a quadrilateral with only two sides parallel?

Ⓐ parallelogram

Ⓑ trapezoid

Ⓒ square

Ⓓ triangle

8 Draw a trapezoid.

List two qualities that describe a trapezoid.

_____

_____

_____

_____

9 Draw a rhombus.

List two qualities that describe a rhombus.

_____

_____

_____

_____

27 Symmetry and Congruence

4.4.4: Identify congruent quadrilaterals and give reasons for congruence using sides, angles, parallels, and perpendiculars.
4.4.5: Identify and draw lines of symmetry in polygons.

Figures With Lines of Symmetry

This is a hexagon with all sides equal in length.

If you fold the hexagon in half, the two halves will match.

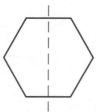 

The line that divides the hexagon in half is called the line of symmetry.

Example 1

How many lines of symmetry does a square have?

STRATEGY: Imagine folding the square exactly in half as many ways as you can.

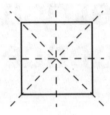

SOLUTION: The dotted lines show that a square has 4 lines of symmetry.

Congruent Figures

Two figures are congruent if they have the same shape and size.

These trapezoids are congruent.

These trapezoids are NOT congruent. They do not have the same size and shape.

Congruent figures do NOT have to be facing the same way. The trapezoids below are congruent. They all have the same shape and size.

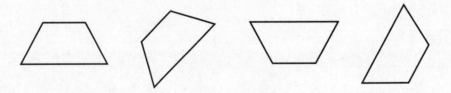

140

Example 2

Which pieces of the puzzle are congruent?

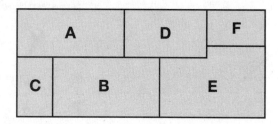

STRATEGY: **Remember what congruent means.**

Find two pieces that are the same shape and size.

SOLUTION: **Rectangles C and F congruent.**

Sample Test Questions

1 Which figure is congruent to this triangle?

Ⓐ

Ⓑ

Ⓒ

Ⓓ

2 How many lines of symmetry does this rectangle have?

Ⓐ 1

Ⓑ 2

Ⓒ 3

Ⓓ 4

3 Which letters have only one line of symmetry each?

X E O M

Ⓐ X and E

Ⓑ X and O

Ⓒ E and O

Ⓓ E and M

4 Which set contains congruent figures?

Ⓐ

Ⓑ

Ⓒ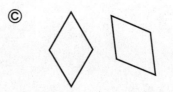

Ⓓ

5 Which figure shows a line of symmetry?

Ⓐ

Ⓑ

Ⓒ

Ⓓ

6 Which shape has exactly four lines of symmetry?

Ⓐ

Ⓑ

Ⓒ

Ⓓ

7 Draw a quadrilateral that has just 2 lines of symmetry. Show the lines of symmetry.

What is the name of your quadrilateral?

_____

28 Three-Dimensional Figures

4.4.6: Construct cubes and prisms and describe their attributes.

Three-dimensional figures are not flat. They have length, width, and height. They are also called solids.

Rectangular Prism

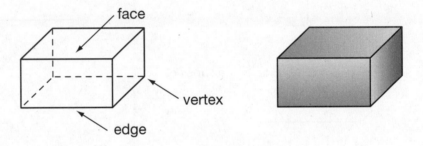

The flat surfaces are called faces. The faces are rectangles.

The faces meet at edges. The edges are line segments.

The edges meet at vertices (plural of vertex).

Cube   A rectangular prism whose faces are squares

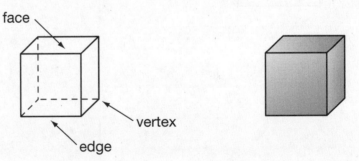

Triangular Prism   A prism with two faces that are triangles

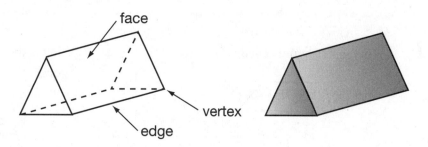

Example 1

How many edges does a rectangular prism have?

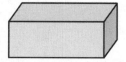

STRATEGY: Count each edge. Don't forget to count the edges you cannot see.

SOLUTION: A rectangular prism has 12 edges.

Example 2

How many faces does a triangular prism have?

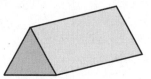

STRATEGY: Count the faces. Don't forget to count the faces you cannot see.

SOLUTION: A triangular prism has 5 faces.

Sample Test Questions

1   What is this figure called?

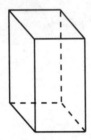

- Ⓐ rectangular prism
- Ⓑ triangular prism
- Ⓒ pyramid
- Ⓓ cube

2   What is the shape of each face of a cube?

- Ⓐ triangle
- Ⓑ square
- Ⓒ pentagon
- Ⓓ hexagon

3   How many edges does this figure have?

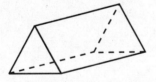

- Ⓐ 6
- Ⓑ 7
- Ⓒ 8
- Ⓓ 9

4   What is the shape of the base of the figure?

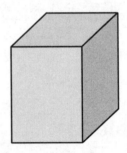

- Ⓐ square
- Ⓑ rectangle
- Ⓒ triangle
- Ⓓ cube

5   What is the name of the figure?

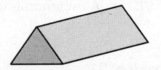

- Ⓐ pyramid
- Ⓑ rectangular prism
- Ⓒ triangular prism
- Ⓓ cube

6 How many more vertices than faces does this figure have?

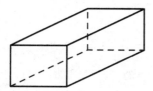

Ⓐ 2

Ⓑ 3

Ⓒ 4

Ⓓ 5

7 How many edges does a cube have?

Ⓐ 8

Ⓑ 12

Ⓒ 14

Ⓓ 16

8 This pattern shows 6 squares. Copy this page, cut along the edges of this diagram, and then fold along the dotted lines. You will find that you have a cube.

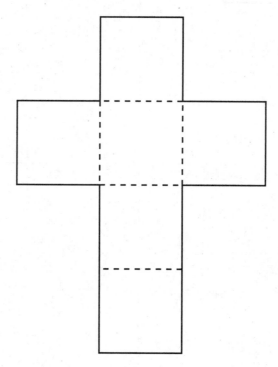

List 3 qualities that all cubes have.

_____

_____

_____

Progress Check for Lessons 24–28

1 Which name describes these figures?

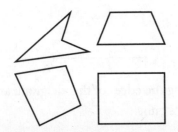

- Ⓐ rectangles
- Ⓑ squares
- Ⓒ quadrilaterals
- Ⓓ hexagons

2 How many faces does a box with rectangular faces have?

- Ⓐ 4
- Ⓑ 6
- Ⓒ 8
- Ⓓ 10

3 Which shows a pair of perpendicular lines?

Ⓐ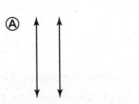

Ⓑ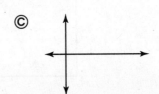

Ⓒ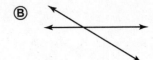

Ⓓ

4 Which figure has exactly two lines of symmetry?

Ⓐ

Ⓑ

Ⓒ

Ⓓ

5 Which figure is congruent to this parallelogram?

Ⓐ

Ⓑ

Ⓒ

Ⓓ

6 What figure does this cereal box resemble?

Ⓐ rectangle

Ⓑ pyramid

Ⓒ cube

Ⓓ rectangular prism

7 Which figure shows a pair of parallel lines?

Ⓐ

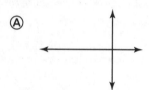

Ⓑ

Ⓒ

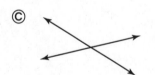

Ⓓ

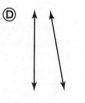

8 What type of angle is shown below?

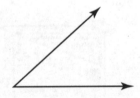

(A) right

(B) acute

(C) scalene

(D) obtuse

9 What is not true about a rectangle?

(A) It has 4 sides.

(B) It has 4 angles.

(C) It can have 2 lines of symmetry.

(D) Two of its angles are acute angles.

10 How many right angles are in this figure?

(A) 4

(B) 6

(C) 7

(D) 8

11 Which figure has exactly four lines of symmetry?

(A) circle

(B) triangle

(C) square

(D) hexagon

12 Which statement is true?

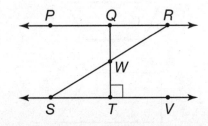

(A) $\overline{PR}$ is parallel to $\overline{SR}$.

(B) $\overline{PR}$ is perpendicular to $\overline{QT}$.

(C) $\overline{QT}$ is parallel to $\overline{SV}$.

(D) $\overline{PR}$ is perpendicular to $\overline{SV}$.

13 What type of angle is shown below?

(A) straight

(B) right

(C) obtuse

(D) acute

14 Which is the best description of a triangular prism?

Ⓐ a three-dimensional figure with faces that are triangles

Ⓑ a three-dimensional figure with 6 faces

Ⓒ a three-dimensional figure with 2 faces that are triangles

Ⓓ a three-dimensional figure with 7 edges

15 Which figure is congruent to this rectangle?

Ⓐ

Ⓑ

Ⓒ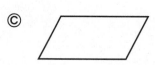

Ⓓ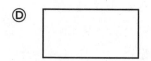

16 Neil wrote this description of a two-dimensional figure.

It is a parallelogram with four right angles.

What figure did Neil describe?

Ⓐ trapezoid

Ⓑ rectangle

Ⓒ quadrilateral

Ⓓ prism

Standard 4: Geometry
Open-Ended Questions

1   Draw an example for each of the following:

   a.   rectangle

   b.   obtuse angle

   c.   acute angle

   d.   two congruent trapezoids

2   Draw a triangle with an obtuse angle.

3   A triangle with one line of symmetry is congruent to a second triangle. Does the second triangle have one line of symmetry? Explain.

_____

_____

_____

_____

_____

4   Use a ruler to draw two rectangles that are congruent.

Standard 5

Measurement

29 Using Rulers

4.5.1: Measure length to the nearest quarter-inch, eighth-inch, and millimeter.

You can use rulers to solve measurement problems.

This is a picture of a centimeter ruler.

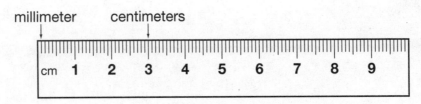

Each whole number on the ruler represents 1 centimeter (cm).

There are 10 millimeters (mm) in each centimeter. Millimeters are shown by the small lines between centimeters.

Example 1

Use the ruler to measure the length of the pen to the nearest millimeter.

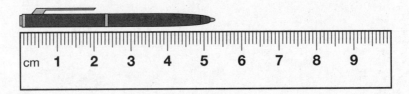

STRATEGY: **Line up the pen with the ruler.**

STEP 1: Notice that one end of the pen is lined up with the end of the ruler.

STEP 2: Count the number of cm and mm to the other end of the pen.

This pen measures 5 cm (50 mm) + 3 mm.

STEP 3:   Add.

50 mm + 3 mm = 53 mm

SOLUTION: **The pen is 53 millimeters (mm) long.**

This is a picture of an inch ruler.

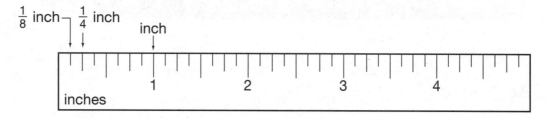

Each whole number on the ruler represents 1 inch (in.).

Note that there are smaller lines in between the whole numbers. Use these lines to measure lengths that are longer or shorter than whole inches. All the lines between the whole numbers can be used to measure lengths to the nearest $\frac{1}{8}$ inch. Use the NEXT longer lines to measure lengths to the nearest $\frac{1}{4}$ inch. The longest lines measure $\frac{1}{2}$ inch, which is the same as $\frac{4}{8}$ or $\frac{2}{4}$ inch.

Example 2

In the box, draw a line segment that is $4\frac{1}{8}$ inches long.

STRATEGY: **Draw from the beginning of the ruler to the mark showing $4\frac{1}{8}$ in.**

STEP 1:   Place your ruler in the box.

STEP 2:   Draw the segment, starting from the left end of the ruler. Draw as far as the number 4 on the ruler.

STEP 3:   Extend the segment $\frac{1}{8}$ inch.

SOLUTION:

Sample Test Questions

1 Use your ruler to measure the length of the pencil to the nearest quarter of an inch.

Ⓐ 5 inches

Ⓑ $5\frac{1}{4}$ inches

Ⓒ $5\frac{1}{2}$ inches

Ⓓ $5\frac{3}{4}$ inches

2 Which line is 26 millimeters long?

Ⓐ ———

Ⓑ ———

Ⓒ ———

Ⓓ ———

3 Use your ruler to measure the length of this line to the nearest $\frac{1}{8}$ inch.

————————

Ⓐ $2\frac{1}{8}$ inches

Ⓑ $2\frac{3}{8}$ inches

Ⓒ $2\frac{5}{8}$ inches

Ⓓ $2\frac{7}{8}$ inches

4 Which line is $1\frac{7}{8}$ inches long?

Ⓐ ──────────────

Ⓑ ────────

Ⓒ ──────────

Ⓓ ───────────

5 Use your ruler to measure the length of this line to the nearest millimeter.

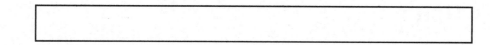

Ⓐ 29 millimeters

Ⓑ 31 millimeters

Ⓒ 33 millimeters

Ⓓ 35 millimeters

6 In the box, draw a line segment that is $3\frac{3}{8}$ inches long.

7 In the box, draw a line segment that is 47 millimeters long.

30 Subtracting Units of Length

4.5.2: Subtract units of length that may require renaming of feet to inches or meters to centimeters.

You can solve some measurement problems by renaming units of length.

Here are several common units of length in both the Customary and the Metric Units.

Customary Units

inch   This segment is 1 inch long. ━━━━━━

foot   This page, from top to bottom, is a little less than 1 foot long.
1 foot (ft) = 12 inches (in.)

Metric Units

centimeter   This segment is 1 centimeter long. ━━
1 centimeter (cm) = 10 millimeters (mm)

meter   A meter is a little longer than 3 feet, or 1 yard.
1 meter (m) = 100 centimeters (cm)

Example 1

Fernando cut a piece of yarn that was 3 feet long. Devin cut a piece of yarn that was 7 inches shorter. How long was the piece of yarn that Devin cut?

STRATEGY: **Rename feet as inches and subtract.**

STEP 1: Rename the amount of yarn Fernando cut.

3 feet = 12 inches + 12 inches + 12 inches

3 feet = 36 inches

STEP 2: Subtract the difference in length of the two pieces of yarn.

36 inches − 7 inches = 29 inches

SOLUTION: **The piece of yarn that Devin cut was 29 inches long. (This length can be renamed as 2 feet 5 inches.)**

Example 2

Norma made a poster for the school book fair. Her poster was 2 meters long. Her friend Dominique made a poster that was 30 centimeters shorter than the poster Norma made. How long was Dominique's poster?

STRATEGY: **Rename meters as centimeters and subtract.**

STEP 1: Rename the length of Norma's poster.

2 meters = 100 centimeters + 100 centimeters

2 meters = 200 centimeters

STEP 2: Subtract the difference in length of the two posters.

200 centimeters − 30 centimeters = 170 centimeters

SOLUTION: **Dominique's poster was 170 centimeters long. (This length can be renamed as 1 meter 70 centimeters.)**

Sample Test Questions

1 The Highland Zoo has two baby boa constrictors. Zoe is 2 feet long. Carmine is 4 inches shorter than Zoe. How long is Carmine?

Ⓐ 26 inches

Ⓑ 24 inches

Ⓒ 20 inches

Ⓓ 16 inches

2 Nathan is wrapping his uncle's birthday gift. He cuts a piece of ribbon that is 2 feet 5 inches long. He realizes that the ribbon is too long and cuts off 6 inches. How long is Nathan's ribbon now?

Ⓐ 19 inches

Ⓑ 21 inches

Ⓒ 23 inches

Ⓓ 29 inches

3 Kimberly measures the door to her classroom. She says the door is 2 meters long. Sharon measures the door and says that it is 1 meter 65 centimeters long. What is the difference between these two measurements?

Ⓐ 1 meter 25 centimeters

Ⓑ 1 meter

Ⓒ 75 centimeters

Ⓓ 35 centimeters

4 Janie's fish tank is 93 centimeters long. Ben's fish tank is 1 meter 45 centimeters long. How much longer is Ben's fish tank?

Ⓐ 145 centimeters

Ⓑ 52 centimeters

Ⓒ 45 centimeters

Ⓓ 7 centimeters

5 Today Darien is using a jump rope that is 8 feet long. He usually uses a jump rope that is 6 feet 8 inches long. How much longer is the jump rope that Darien is using today?

Ⓐ 1 foot 4 inches

Ⓑ 1 foot 8 inches

Ⓒ 2 feet

Ⓓ 2 feet 4 inches

6 Ava needs 6 feet of rope for her science project. She has 37 inches of rope. How much more rope does Ava need? Show your work.

162

31 Perimeter and Area

4.5.3: Know and use formulas for finding the perimeters of rectangles and squares.
4.5.4: Know and use formulas for finding the areas of rectangles and squares.
4.5.5: Estimate and calculate the area of rectangular shapes using appropriate units such as square centimeter (cm^2), square meter (m^2), square inch (in.^{2}), or square yard (yd^2).
4.5.6: Understand that rectangles with the same area can have different perimeters and that rectangles with the same perimeter can have different areas.
4.5.7: Find areas of shapes by dividing them into basic shapes such as rectangles.

Perimeter of a Polygon

A polygon is any closed figure formed by line segments. Examples of polygons are triangles, rectangles, pentagons, and hexagons.

The perimeter of a polygon is the distance around the polygon.

> **RULE:**   To find the perimeter of a polygon, add the lengths of the sides.

You can use formulas to find the perimeter (P = perimeter) of some polygons.

Rectangle

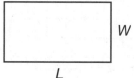

$P = 2L + 2W$ or $P = 2(L + W)$
or $P = L + L + W + W$
(L = length and W = width)

Square

$P = 4s$ (s = length of a side)
or $P = s + s + s + s$

Area

The area of a figure is the number of square units needed to cover it.

Example 1

What is the area of this rectangle? Each small square is 1 square unit.

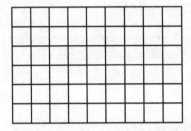

STRATEGY: **Find the number of square units in the rectangle.**

    STEP 1: Count the number of rows.

            There are 6 rows.

    STEP 2: Count the number of columns.

            There are 9 columns.

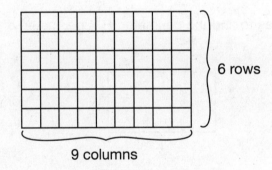

    STEP 3: Multiply the rows by the columns.

            $6 \times 9 = 54$ squares.

SOLUTION: **The area is 54 square units.**

You can use formulas to find the area (A = area) of some polygons.

Rectangle

$A = L \times W$ (where L = length and W = width)

W

L

Square

$A = s^2$ (where s = side)
s^2 is the same as $s \times s$

s

s

Example 2

A rectangular table measures 6 feet by 4 feet. What is the area of the table?

STRATEGY: **Use the formula for the area of a rectangle.**

STEP 1: Write the formula.

$A = LW$

STEP 2: Substitute the table's length and width into the formula.

$A = LW = 6 \times 4 = 24$

STEP 3: Write the answer in square units.

(Area is measured in square units: square feet (ft^2), square centimeters (cm^2), etc. In this case, the area is measured in square feet.)

SOLUTION: **The area of the table is 24 square feet.**

Example 3

Use your ruler to draw a rectangle with length of 5 cm and width of 2 cm. Find the perimeter of the rectangle.

STRATEGY: **Use the formula for perimeter of rectangles.**

STEP 1: Draw the rectangle.

One side of the rectangle measures 5 cm. The other side of the rectangle measures 2 cm.

STEP 2: Find the perimeter of the rectangle.

Use the formula for finding perimeter.

$P = 2L + 2W$

$P = 2 \times 5 + 2 \times 2$

$P = 10 + 4$

$P = 14$ cm

SOLUTION: **The rectangle has a perimeter of 14 centimeters.**

Sample Test Questions

1 What is the perimeter of this figure?

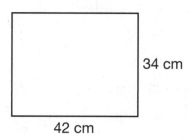

34 cm

42 cm

Ⓐ 1,428 cm

Ⓑ 168 cm

Ⓒ 152 cm

Ⓓ 136 cm

2 What is the formula for finding the perimeter of a rectangle?

Ⓐ $P = 2 \times \text{length} + \text{width}$

Ⓑ $P = \text{length} + 2 \times \text{width}$

Ⓒ $P = 2 \times \text{length} + 2 \times \text{width}$

Ⓓ $P = \text{length} \times \text{width}$

3 What is the area of the shaded section?

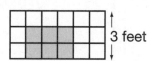

3 feet

Ⓐ 3 ft^2

Ⓑ 6 ft^2

Ⓒ 9 ft^2

Ⓓ 12 ft^2

4 What is the area of a square with a side 10 cm long?

Ⓐ 20 cm

Ⓑ 40 square cm

Ⓒ 100 square cm

Ⓓ 200 square cm

5 What is the area of this figure?

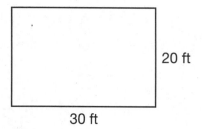

20 ft

30 ft

Ⓐ 60 square feet

Ⓑ 100 square feet

Ⓒ 400 square feet

Ⓓ 600 square feet

6 What is the perimeter of a square with sides measuring 14 inches?

Ⓐ 56 inches

Ⓑ 66 inches

Ⓒ 96 inches

Ⓓ 196 inches

7 How many square-foot tiles would it take to cover the floor in this plan?

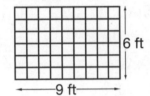

6 ft

9 ft

Ⓐ 54 tiles

Ⓑ 64 tiles

Ⓒ 81 tiles

Ⓓ 108 tiles

8 What is the area of the figure?

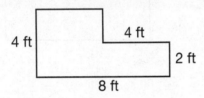

4 ft

4 ft

2 ft

8 ft

Ⓐ 20 square feet

Ⓑ 24 square feet

Ⓒ 30 square feet

Ⓓ 32 square feet

9 Shawn uses a desk that is 30 inches long and 25 inches wide. Taylor uses a desk that is twice as long and twice as wide. What is the perimeter of Taylor's desk in inches?

Ⓐ 85

Ⓑ 110

Ⓒ 160

Ⓓ 220

10 The length of the fence on one side of Mr. Smith's rectangular garden is 8 feet. The perimeter of the garden is 28 feet. What is the area of the garden?

Ⓐ 24 ft^2

Ⓑ 36 ft^2

Ⓒ 48 ft^2

Ⓓ 64 ft^2

11 This is a diagram of Mr. Frankel's classroom. What is the area of the classroom?

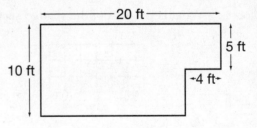

20 ft

5 ft

10 ft

4 ft

12 Use your ruler to draw two rectangles that have the same area but different perimeters.

Rectangle A

Rectangle B

Area: _____

Area: _____

Perimeter: _____

Perimeter: _____

32 Introduction to Volume and Capacity

4.5.8: Use volume and capacity as different ways of measuring the space inside a shape.

The volume of a three-dimensional figure can be measured by counting the number of cubes it takes to fill the space. For this lesson, you may want to use blocks to help you calculate volume.

Example 1

How many cubes (or blocks) will it take to build this figure?

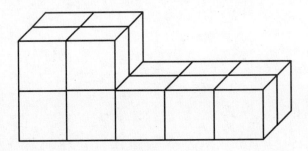

STRATEGY: **Count each level and add.**

STEP 1: Count the cubes on the bottom level.

There are 2 rows. Each row has 5 cubes. So there are 10 cubes in all.

STEP 2: Count the top level of cubes.

There are 2 rows of 2 cubes each—4 in all.

STEP 3: Add the two levels.

SOLUTION: **10 + 4 = 14 cubes.**

Example 2

Find the volume of this box.

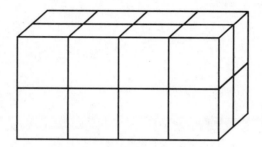

STRATEGY: **Count the number of cubes that fill the box.**

STEP 1: Count the number of cubes on the top layer.

There are 2 rows of 4 cubes each—8 cubes in all.

STEP 2: How many cubes are in the bottom layer?

There are as many cubes in the bottom layer as in the top layer—8 cubes.

STEP 3: Add.

8 + 8 = 16

SOLUTION: **The volume of the box is 16 cubes.**

Capacity is another way to measure the space inside a shape. The capacity of an object is the amount of liquid it can hold. Here are some units used to measure capacity.

cup: the size of a small carton of milk (like the kind you get in school)

pint: 2 cups

quart: 2 pints

gallon: 4 quarts

Example 3

Bruce poured a small glass of juice to drink with his breakfast.
Which is the most likely amount of juice Bruce poured?

Ⓐ gallon

Ⓑ quart

Ⓒ pint

Ⓓ cup

STRATEGY: **Think about the different units of capacity.**

   STEP 1:   The question says that Bruce poured a small glass of juice.

   It is not likely that Bruce poured a gallon or a quart of juice to drink with his breakfast.

   STEP 2:   Look at the picture of the juice glass.

   The glass does not look big enough to hold a pint, or 2 cups, of juice.

   STEP 3:   Think about the size of the cup. A cup is about the same as a container of milk you would get at school.

   It seems likely that Bruce poured this amount of juice.

SOLUTION: **Bruce probably poured a cup of juice.**

Sample Test Questions

1 How many cubes would it take to build this figure?

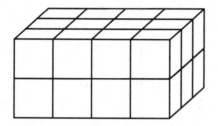

Ⓐ 16 cubes

Ⓑ 18 cubes

Ⓒ 20 cubes

Ⓓ 24 cubes

2 How many cubes were used to build this figure?

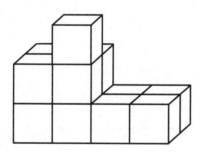

Ⓐ 13 cubes

Ⓑ 12 cubes

Ⓒ 11 cubes

Ⓓ 10 cubes

3 Cyrus needs to fill his new fish tank with water. Which is a reasonable estimate for the amount of water the fish tank will hold?

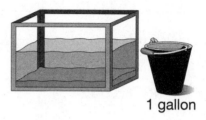

1 gallon

Ⓐ 6 gallons

Ⓑ 6 quarts

Ⓒ 6 pints

Ⓓ 6 cups

4 Find the volume of this cube.

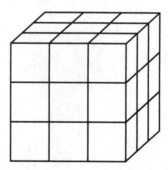

Ⓐ 9 cubes

Ⓑ 18 cubes

Ⓒ 27 cubes

Ⓓ 30 cubes

5 How many more cubes will it take to make the top layer of the figure match the bottom layer?

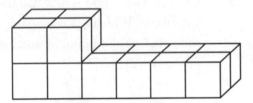

Ⓐ 6 cubes

Ⓑ 5 cubes

Ⓒ 8 cubes

Ⓓ 7 cubes

6 Coral has a bouquet of flowers. She filled a vase for her flowers. Which of the following is a reasonable estimate for the amount of water the vase holds?

Ⓐ 4 fluid ounces

Ⓑ 4 pints

Ⓒ 4 quarts

Ⓓ 4 gallons

7 What is the volume of this figure?

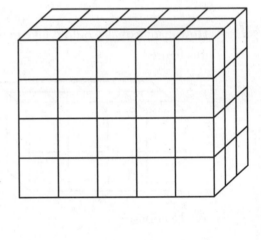

_____

Explain how you found the volume of the figure.

_____

_____

_____

_____

_____

33 Equivalent Time Periods

4.5.9: Add time intervals involving hours and minutes.

You can solve some time problems by renaming units of time.

1 minute = 60 seconds

1 hour = 60 minutes

Example 1

Daryl swims the same amount of time each day. If he swims 2 hours 27 minutes in a week, how many minutes does he swim each day?

STRATEGY: **Rename the total time as minutes.**

  STEP 1:   Rename 2 hours 27 minutes.

  1 hour = 60 minutes

  2 hours = 2 × 60 = 120 minutes

  120 + 27 = 147 minutes

  STEP 2:   Divide by the number of days in a week.

  $\frac{147}{7} = 21$

SOLUTION: **Daryl swims 21 minutes each day.**

Example 2

Bob saw a movie that lasted 130 minutes. How many hours and minutes was the movie?

STRATEGY: **Remember, there are 60 minutes in an hour.**

        STEP 1: How many minutes are in 1 hour?

                There are 60 minutes in 1 hour.

        STEP 2: How many full hours are in 130 minutes?

                Subtract an hour (60 minutes) from 130 minutes.

130	minutes	→	time of movie
− 60	minutes in 1 hour		
70	minutes left over	→	more than 1 hour

        STEP 3: Subtract another 60 minutes (for a total of 2 hours).

70	minutes left over	→	more than 1 hour
− 60	minutes in 1 hour		
10	minutes left over	→	less than 1 hour

                2 hours 10 minutes = 130 minutes

SOLUTION: **The movie was 2 hours 10 minutes long.**

Sample Test Questions

1 Which is the same as 1 hour 20 minutes?

Ⓐ 60 minutes

Ⓑ 70 minutes

Ⓒ 80 minutes

Ⓓ 90 minutes

2 How many minutes is Philip in school if he spends 6 hours there?

Ⓐ 240 minutes

Ⓑ 250 minutes

Ⓒ 300 minutes

Ⓓ 360 minutes

3 Tammy's book club meets for 45 minutes each week. How many hours and minutes does Tammy's book club meet in 6 weeks?

Ⓐ 3 hours 30 minutes

Ⓑ 4 hours 10 minutes

Ⓒ 4 hours 30 minutes

Ⓓ 4 hours 45 minutes

4 Felice babysat for 2 hours 50 minutes. Which is equal to 2 hours 50 minutes?

Ⓐ 110 minutes

Ⓑ 150 minutes

Ⓒ 170 minutes

Ⓓ 210 minutes

5 Which is equal to 210 minutes?

Ⓐ 2 hours 30 minutes

Ⓑ 3 hours

Ⓒ 3 hours 30 minutes

Ⓓ 4 hours

6 Martha spent 2 hours 20 minutes painting. How many minutes did Martha spend painting?

Ⓐ 80 minutes

Ⓑ 120 minutes

Ⓒ 140 minutes

Ⓓ 180 minutes

7 Which is equal to 3 hours 40 minutes?

Ⓐ 180 minutes

Ⓑ 220 minutes

Ⓒ 260 minutes

Ⓓ 340 minutes

8 Corinna participated in her school's walkathon. She walked for 270 minutes. How long did Corinna walk in hours and minutes? Show your work.

_____

177

34 Determining the Amount of Change

4.5.10: Determine the amount of change from a purchase.

You can solve money problems involving change the same way you subtract decimals. (See Lesson 15.)

Example

Peter bought a notebook and a pen that cost $3.24. He paid with $4.00. How much change did he get?

STRATEGY: **Subtract money amounts the same way you subtract decimals.**

> **STEP 1:** Write the subtraction problem vertically. Remember to line up the decimal points.
>
> $$\begin{array}{r} \$4.00 \\ -\ 3.24 \\ \hline \end{array}$$
>
> **STEP 2:** Subtract the total cost from $4.00 to find the change.
>
> $$\begin{array}{rl} \$4.00 & \text{amount paid} \\ -\ 3.24 & \text{total cost} \\ \hline \$0.76 & \text{change} \end{array}$$

SOLUTION: **The change is $0.76, or 76 cents.**

Sample Test Questions

1 Vicky bought a toy truck for $4.26. How much change will she get if she pays with 5 dollars?

Ⓐ 76 cents

Ⓑ 74 cents

Ⓒ 26 cents

Ⓓ 24 cents

2 Michael's new puzzle cost $6.45. He paid with a $10 bill. How much change did he get?

Ⓐ $16.45

Ⓑ $5.55

Ⓒ $4.45

Ⓓ $3.55

3 Julio spent $4.28 on art supplies. He paid with a $5 bill. How much change did he get?

Ⓐ $0.72

Ⓑ $0.82

Ⓒ $1.72

Ⓓ $9.28

4 Carmen bought a magazine that cost $2.60. She paid with a $10 bill. How much change did she get?

Ⓐ $7.20

Ⓑ $7.40

Ⓒ $8.40

Ⓓ $12.60

5 Seth bought a paperback book that cost $7.29. How much change did he get if he paid for the book with a $10 bill?

Ⓐ $17.29

Ⓑ $7.29

Ⓒ $3.81

Ⓓ $2.71

6 Arthur bought cat food for his new kitten. The food cost $6.09. Arthur paid with a $10 bill. How much change did Arthur get? Show your work.

_____

Progress Check for
Lessons 29–34

1 Felita found a baby spider crawling on her arm. She used her centimeter ruler to measure it.

What was the length of the baby spider to the nearest millimeter?

Ⓐ 10 millimeters

Ⓑ 11 millimeters

Ⓒ 12 millimeters

Ⓓ 13 millimeters

2 Stella measured the height of her front door. It was 2 yards (1 yard = 3 feet). What was the height of Stella's front door in inches?

Ⓐ 24 inches

Ⓑ 36 inches

Ⓒ 48 inches

Ⓓ 72 inches

3 What is the perimeter of this figure?

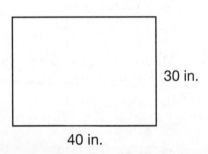

30 in.

40 in.

Ⓐ 70 inches

Ⓑ 100 inches

Ⓒ 120 inches

Ⓓ 140 inches

4 How many cubes make up this three-dimensional figure?

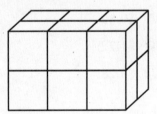

Ⓐ 9 cubes

Ⓑ 10 cubes

Ⓒ 12 cubes

Ⓓ 16 cubes

5 What measure does the arrow point to?

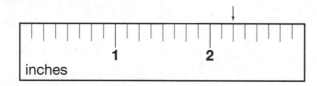

Ⓐ 2 inches

Ⓒ $2\frac{1}{2}$ inches

Ⓑ $2\frac{1}{4}$ inches

Ⓓ $2\frac{3}{4}$ inches

6 Use a centimeter ruler to find the length of this pencil.

Ⓐ 20 millimeters

Ⓑ 50 millimeters

Ⓒ 80 millimeters

Ⓓ 100 millimeters

7 The perimeter of a square is 44 m. What is the length of each side?

Ⓐ 8 mm

Ⓑ 10 mm

Ⓒ 11 mm

Ⓓ 121 mm

8 What is the area of the figure shown below?

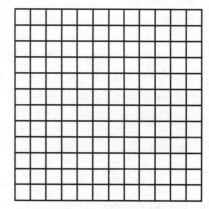

Each ☐ = 1 square inch

Ⓐ 12 square inches

Ⓑ 24 square inches

Ⓒ 120 square inches

Ⓓ 144 square inches

9 What is the area of this figure?

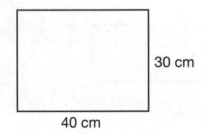

30 cm

40 cm

Ⓐ 70 cm²

Ⓑ 149 cm²

Ⓒ 1200 cm²

Ⓓ 2400 cm²

10 Mariel bought ingredients for cupcakes. She spent $5.04. She paid with a $10 bill. How much change did Mariel get?

Ⓐ $15.04

Ⓑ $5.96

Ⓒ $5.04

Ⓓ $4.96

11 Eduardo is filling his sister's wading pool. Which is the most likely amount of water that Eduardo needs?

Ⓐ 30 cups

Ⓑ 30 pints

Ⓒ 30 quarts

Ⓓ 30 gallons

12 Debra watched a television show that lasted 135 minutes. How long was the television show in hours and minutes?

Ⓐ 1 hour 35 minutes

Ⓑ 2 hours 5 minutes

Ⓒ 2 hours 15 minutes

Ⓓ 2 hours 35 minutes

13 Frankie had a piece of string that was 3 feet long. Then he cut 8 inches off the string. How much string did he have left?

Ⓐ 83 inches

Ⓑ 38 inches

Ⓒ 32 inches

Ⓓ 28 inches

14 Ramon spends $1.07 at the store. He gives the cashier a $5 bill. How much change does Ramon get back?

Ⓐ $3.03

Ⓑ $3.93

Ⓒ $4.07

Ⓓ $6.07

15 Carlise had a piece of licorice that was 4 feet long. Carlise and her friend ate 18 inches of the licorice. How much licorice was left?

Ⓐ 48 inches

Ⓑ 40 inches

Ⓒ 38 inches

Ⓓ 30 inches

16 What is the volume of the figure shown below?

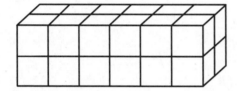

Ⓐ 24 cubes

Ⓑ 26 cubes

Ⓒ 28 cubes

Ⓓ 32 cubes

17 Beatrice did homework for 170 minutes. How long is that in hours and minutes?

Ⓐ 1 hour 70 minutes

Ⓑ 2 hours 10 minutes

Ⓒ 2 hours 50 minutes

Ⓓ 2 hours 70 minutes

18 Nicki bought food for her dog. She spent $3.78 and paid with a $10 bill. How much change did she get back?

Ⓐ $5.32

Ⓑ $6.22

Ⓒ $7.72

Ⓓ $13.78

19 Sherry and her friend went white-water rafting. They were on the water for 230 minutes. How long is that in hours and minutes?

Ⓐ 4 hours 10 minutes

Ⓑ 3 hours 50 minutes

Ⓒ 3 hours 10 minutes

Ⓓ 2 hours 50 minutes

Standard 5: Measurement
Open-Ended Questions

1   Use a centimeter ruler to draw a rectangle 6 centimeters long and 4 centimeters wide.

What is the perimeter of the rectangle?

_____

What is the area of the rectangle?

_____

2 Patrice is drawing a rectangle with an area equal to 12 square inches.

Draw a rectangle with an area equal to 12 square inches. Label the lengths of each side of your rectangle. Your rectangle does not have to be drawn to scale.

3 This diagram shows the outline of a school playground. Find the area of the playground.

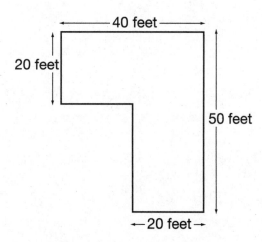

4 Horatio measured a piece of yarn that was 5 feet long. Then he cut 27 inches off the yarn. How much yarn did he have left? Show your work.

Standard 6

Data Analysis and Probability

35 | Bar Graphs

4.6.2: Interpret data graphs to answer questions about a situation.
4.6.3: Summarize and display the results of probability experiments in a clear and organized way.

A graph is a way to show and compare numerical information, or data.

Bar graphs use bars of different heights to compare data.

Example 1

The graph shows how many books were read by 4 children in the fifth grade. Who read the most books? How many did that person read?

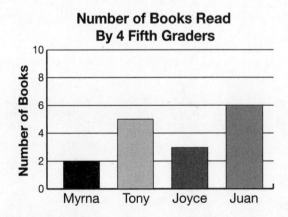

STRATEGY: **Find the highest bar. Then look at the scale to the left. Read the number that is even with the top of the highest bar.**

STEP 1: Look at all the bars. Which one is highest?

The highest bar is the one for Juan.

STEP 2: From the top of Juan's bar, draw a line to the number on the left.

It tells you the number of books Juan read.

STEP 3:   Read the number from the scale.

The line for Juan's bar is 6.

SOLUTION: Juan read the most books. He read 6 books.

Example 2

Colleen collected information about the number of sunny days last spring. This is what she found out.

April had 14 sunny days.

May had 18 sunny days.

June had 20 sunny days.

Create a bar graph that shows the information Colleen collected.

STRATEGY: Follow these steps for making a bar graph.

STEP 1:   Draw the horizontal and vertical axes.

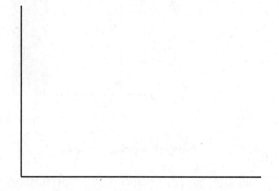

STEP 2:   Choose a scale for the vertical axis. Label it.

Counting by 2's is a good idea.

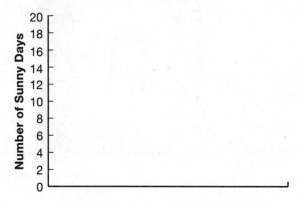

STEP 3:   Write the categories for the horizontal axis. Label the axis.

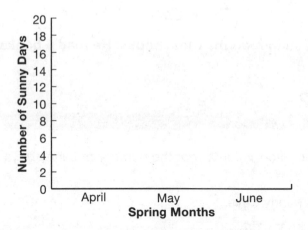

STEP 4:   Look at the data Colleen collected. Use it to draw bars for each month. Remember the scale.

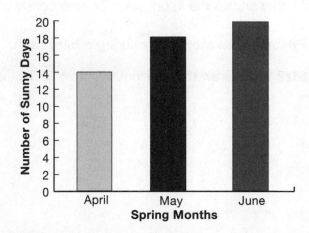

STEP 5:   Give the graph a title.

SOLUTION: **This bar graph shows the information Colleen collected.**

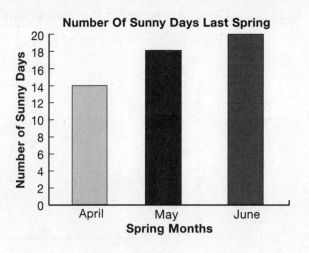

Sample Test Questions

These bar graphs show spelling-test scores in December and June. Use the graphs to answer Questions 1–3.

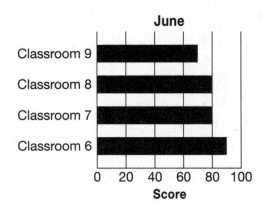

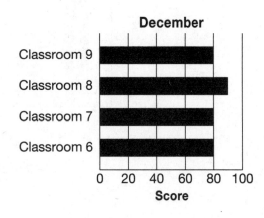

1 What was the spelling score of Classroom 8 in December?

Ⓐ 60

Ⓑ 70

Ⓒ 80

Ⓓ 90

2 What was the spelling score of Classroom 9 in June?

Ⓐ 60

Ⓑ 70

Ⓒ 80

Ⓓ 90

3 In which classroom did the children do better on the spelling test in June than in December?

Ⓐ Classroom 6

Ⓑ Classroom 7

Ⓒ Classroom 8

Ⓓ Classroom 9

This bar graph shows how much water Lynne drank last week. Use the graph to answer Questions 4–6.

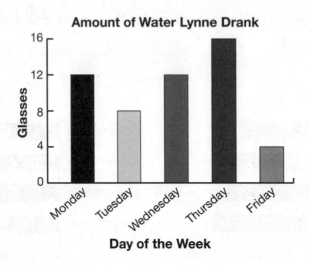

4 How many glasses of water did Lynne drink on Monday?

Ⓐ 3 glasses

Ⓑ 6 glasses

Ⓒ 8 glasses

Ⓓ 12 glasses

5 How many more glasses of water did Lynne drink on Thursday than on Tuesday?

Ⓐ 16 glasses

Ⓑ 12 glasses

Ⓒ 10 glasses

Ⓓ 8 glasses

6 How many glasses of water did Lynne drink on Thursday and Friday altogether?

Ⓐ 5 glasses

Ⓑ 8 glasses

Ⓒ 16 glasses

Ⓓ 20 glasses

7 Mark collected information about the kinds of pets that the fifth graders in his school have. He found the following information:

10 students have birds.   30 students have dogs.

20 students have fish.   50 students have cats.

In the space below, create a bar graph that shows the information that Mark collected. Remember to include a title and label the side and bottom axes.

8 Jen works at an ice-cream parlor. One day, she collected information about people's favorite ice-cream flavors. This is what Jen has found:

25 people like chocolate.

40 people like strawberry.

55 people like vanilla.

In the space below, create a bar graph that shows Jen's information. Use a scale that goes by 5's for your graph. Remember to include a title and labels for your bar graph.

36 | Tables

4.6.1: Represent data on a number line and in tables, including frequency tables.

A table can help you organize information.

Example 1

This table shows how a group of fifth-graders gets to school.

How Fifth-Graders Get to School

Walk	‖‖‖ ‖‖‖ ‖‖‖ ‖‖‖ ‖‖‖ ‖‖‖							
Bus	‖‖‖ ‖‖‖ ‖‖‖ ‖‖‖ ‖‖‖ ‖‖‖ ‖‖‖ ‖‖‖ ‖‖‖
Car	‖‖‖ ‖‖‖ ‖‖‖

How many students get to school by walking?

NOTICE: This chart uses tallies, which are marks that show numbers.

‖‖‖ means the number 3.   ‖‖‖ means the number 5.

STRATEGY: **Count the tallies in the row for walking.**

     STEP 1: Find the row for walking.

         The first row shows the number of students who walk to school.

     STEP 2: Count the tallies in the first row.

         Remember, ‖‖‖ means 5 students, so you can count by 5's: 5, 10, 15, 20. Now count on the 1's: 21, 22, 23.

SOLUTION: **23 students walk to school.**

Example 2

Nick, Nancy, Peggy, and Grace went bird watching last week. They kept track of the number of birds they saw.

Nick saw 8 birds.

Nancy saw 14 birds.

Peggy saw 12 birds.

Grace saw 9 birds.

How can the friends use a table to show this information?

STRATEGY: **Follow the steps for making a table.**

STEP 1:   Choose a title for the table.

The table will be about the number of birds seen, so "Number of Birds Seen" is a good title.

STEP 2:   Decide whether to use numbers or tallies for the table.

Numbers are given, so use them.

STEP 3:   Set up the table.

Make sure there is a row for each person.

Make sure there are two columns. There should be one column for names and one column for the number of birds each person saw.

Fill in the table. Remember to leave room for the title.

SOLUTION: **This table shows the number of birds the friends saw.**

Number of Birds Seen

Nick	8
Nancy	14
Peggy	12
Grace	9

Example 3

Coach Jensen kept track of swimmers' lap times at practice. This table shows what he found.

Swimmers' Times

Time	Number of Swimmers
40-44 seconds	3
45-49 seconds	8
50-54 seconds	6
55-59 seconds	5

How many swimmers swam a lap in 45-49 seconds?

STRATEGY: **Use the table to find the information.**

STEP 1: Find the row for 45-49 seconds.

STEP 2: Run your finger across to find the number of swimmers who had that time.

8 swimmers had that time.

SOLUTION: **8 swimmers swam a lap in 45-49 seconds.**

Sample Test Questions

This table shows some common names of some students in Central City School. Use the table for Questions 1–3.

Common Names at Central City School

Michael	⊦⊦⊦⊦ ⊦⊦⊦⊦ ⊦⊦⊦⊦ ⊦⊦⊦⊦ ⊦⊦⊦⊦ ||
Ashley	⊦⊦⊦⊦ ⊦⊦⊦⊦ ⊦⊦⊦⊦ ⊦⊦⊦⊦ ||
José	⊦⊦⊦⊦ ⊦⊦⊦⊦ ⊦⊦⊦⊦ ||
Brittany	⊦⊦⊦⊦ ⊦⊦⊦⊦ ⊦⊦⊦⊦ ⊦⊦⊦⊦ |||

1 How many students are named Michael?

Ⓐ 6

Ⓑ 27

Ⓒ 30

Ⓓ 40

2 How many more students are named Michael than Ashley?

Ⓐ 5

Ⓑ 10

Ⓒ 12

Ⓓ 22

3 How many more students are named Brittany than José?

Ⓐ 1

Ⓑ 3

Ⓒ 5

Ⓓ 6

Each student in Ms. Michael's class counted the number of peanuts in his or her bag. This table shows the results of their experiment. Use the table for Questions 4 and 5.

Number of Peanuts in a Bag

Number of Peanuts	Number of Bags
20-24	1
25-29	6
30-34	3
35-39	8
40-44	3

4 How many bags had 30 to 34 peanuts?

Ⓐ 8

Ⓑ 6

Ⓒ 3

Ⓓ 1

5 How many bags had 35 to 44 peanuts?

Ⓐ 3

Ⓑ 6

Ⓒ 8

Ⓓ 11

6 A fifth-grade teacher at Maplewood Elementary School measured the heights of some of the students in the fifth grade. This is what she found.

27 students were 48 inches tall.

16 students were 51 inches tall.

36 students were 53 inches tall.

43 students were 54 inches tall.

In the space below, create a table that shows this information. Use tally marks in your table.

7 Alejandro visited a dog park every day for a month and counted the number of different kinds of dogs. This is what he saw.

43 Jack Russell terriers

34 German shepherds

16 poodles

22 golden retrievers

In the space below, create a table that shows this information. Use numbers in your table.

37 Line Plots

4.6.2: Interpret data graphs to answer questions about a situation.
4.6.3: Summarize and display the results of probability experiments in a clear and organized way.

Line plots are a useful and quick way to display sets of data. Line plots are related to number lines.

Example 1

This line plot shows the heights of trees in a park.

Height (ft) of Trees in Braddock Park

```
                        X
            X           X   X               X
    X   X           X   X               X   X
    X   X           X   X   X           X   X   X   X
   ────────────────────────────────────────────────
    20  21  22  23  24  25  26  27  28  29  30
```

What is the height of the greatest number of trees?

STRATEGY: **Find the column with the greatest number of X's.**

STEP 1: Compare the number of X's for each of the tree heights.

0 X's:	22 ft, 26 ft
1 X:	25 ft, 29 ft, 30 ft
2 X's:	20 ft, 28 ft
3 X's:	21 ft, 24 ft, 27 ft
4 X's:	23 ft

STEP 2: Find the column with the greatest number of X's.

The column for 23 ft has the greatest number of X's. It has 4 X's.

This means that 4 of the trees in Braddock Park were 23 ft tall.

SOLUTION: **The height of the greatest number of trees is 23 ft.**

Example 2

This line plot shows the height (in inches) of the players on a fifth-grade girls' basketball team.

Height (in.) of Players on Basketball Team

```
                                  X
                        X         X
              X         X         X
              X         X         X
            X   X       X   X   X   X
        _____
        30  32  34  36  38  40  42  44  46  48  50  52
```

How many players are taller than 40 inches?

STRATEGY: Locate 40 inches on the number line.

STEP 1: Place your finger at the 40-inch mark on the line.

STEP 2: List the number of X's to the right of the 40-inch mark.

42 inches: 4 X's
44 inches: 1 X
46 inches: 5 X's
48 inches: 1 X

STEP 3: Add.

4 + 1 + 5 + 1 = 11

SOLUTION: **11 players are taller than 40 inches.**

You can collect data by conducting a survey. When you conduct a survey, you ask people a question or questions. You can record the answers in a table or a line plot.

Example 3

Ms. Khoury's class conducted a survey to find out how many siblings each student has. The table below shows what they found.

Number of siblings	0	1	2	3	4	5	6
Number of students	2	3	5	5	2	0	1

Make a line plot that shows the data.

STRATEGY: **Follow these steps.**

STEP 1: Choose a title for the line plot.

The title should describe the survey. "Number of Siblings that Students in Ms. Khoury's Class Have" is a good title.

STEP 2: Set up the numbers for the line plot.

**Number of Siblings that
Students in Ms. Khoury's Class Have**

```
   0   1   2   3   4   5   6
            Siblings
```

STEP 3: Make an X for each student.

The table will tell you how many X's to make for each number.

- 2 students have no siblings. Put 2 X's above the 0.
- 3 students have 1 sibling. Put 3 X's above the 1.
- 5 students have 2 siblings. Put 5 X's above the 2.
- 5 students have 3 siblings. Put 5 X's above the 3.
- 2 students have 4 siblings. Put 2 X's above the 4.
- 0 students have 5 siblings. Do not put any X's above the 5.
- 1 student has 6 siblings. Put 1 X above the 6.

SOLUTION:

**Number of Siblings that
Students in Ms. Khoury's Class Have**

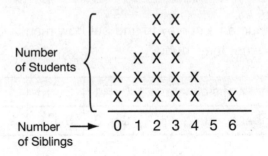

Number
of Students

```
                X  X
                X  X
             X  X  X
          X  X  X  X  X
          X  X  X  X  X     X
         _____
          0  1  2  3  4  5  6
```

Number →
of Siblings

Sample Test Questions

Use the line plot to answer Questions 1–4.

Height of Sunflowers in Marissa's Garden

```
                          X
          X  X       X  X
       X  X  X  X    X  X       X
       X  X  X  X    X  X       X       X
      ─────────────────────────────────────
       55 56 57 58 59 60 61 62 63 64 65
                     Inches
```

1 What is the height of the greatest number of sunflowers?

Ⓐ 56 inches

Ⓑ 57 inches

Ⓒ 60 inches

Ⓓ 61 inches

2 What is the height of the tallest sunflower in the garden?

Ⓐ 57 inches

Ⓑ 60 inches

Ⓒ 61 inches

Ⓓ 65 inches

3 What is the range of heights of sunflowers?

Ⓐ 10 inches

Ⓑ 20 inches

Ⓒ 59 inches

Ⓓ 60 inches

4 How many sunflowers are 62 inches tall?

Ⓐ 0

Ⓑ 1

Ⓒ 3

Ⓓ 4

5 A number line is part of which type of graph?

Ⓐ bar graph

Ⓑ line plot

Ⓒ circle graph

Ⓓ pictograph

6 Students in Mrs. Gregory's class made a line plot of the number of magazines that families receive in their homes regularly.

Number of Magazines Received by Students' Families

```
    X
X   X   X
X   X   X   X           X   X
X   X   X   X       X   X   X
X   X   X   X   X   X   X   X
————————————————————————————————
0   1   2   3   4   5   6   7   8   9   10
```
Magazines

How many families receive 3 or fewer magazines regularly?

Ⓐ 11

Ⓑ 13

Ⓒ 15

Ⓓ 16

7 The table below shows fifth-grade students' scores on a science test.

Scores	70	75	80	85	90	95	100
Number of Students	12	11	4	21	17	22	13

Use the information given in the table to make a line plot.

204

38 Displaying Probability Experiments

4.6.3: Summarize and display the results of probability experiments in a clear and organized way.

The probability of an event tells us how likely the event is to take place. You can show the data of a probability experiment in a table or graph. It is important to show the data set you have collected so that it can be studied and predictions can be made.

Example

Students in Mr. McCormick's class performed a probability experiment with this spinner.

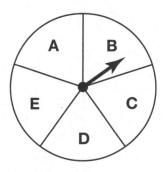

They spun the spinner 20 times. These are their results.

Spinner Results

Letter	Number of Times Landed On
A	4
B	3
C	5
D	2
E	6

Draw a bar graph to show the results of the spinner experiment.

STRATEGY: Follow the steps you learned in Lesson 35 to draw a bar graph.

SOLUTION: This bar graph shows the results of the spinner experiment.

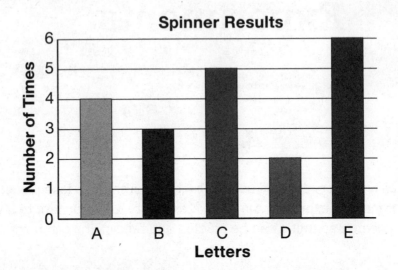

Sample Test Questions

1 Roll a number cube 36 times. Use a table to record the number of times that 1, 2, 3, 4, 5, and 6 appear. Draw a bar graph to show your results.

3 Roll two number cubes 50 times. Add the two numbers after each roll. Create a table to record the results. Then draw a line plot that displays the results shown in the table. (The line will be marked from 2 to 12.)

2 Construct a spinner that has four equal parts. Label the parts A, B, C, and D. Spin the spinner 40 times. Use a table to record the number of times that A, B, C, and D appear. Draw a bar graph to show your results.

Progress Check for
Lessons 35–38

This graph shows the results of a vote taken in Jeff's fifth-grade class. Students were asked what sport they wanted to play in gym class.

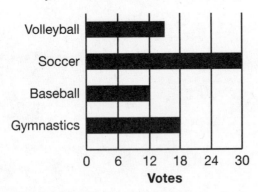

Sports Students Wanted to Play

1 How many more students voted for soccer than for gymnastics?

Ⓐ 12

Ⓑ 18

Ⓒ 28

Ⓓ 30

2 How many students voted for baseball and volleyball altogether?

Ⓐ 21

Ⓑ 25

Ⓒ 27

Ⓓ 30

This bar graph shows the number of newspapers and magazines sold at a corner store over four weekends. Use it to answer Questions 3 and 4.

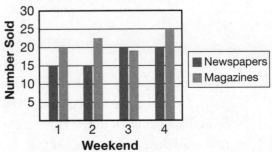

Newspapers and Magazines Sold at the Corner Store

3 During which weekend were more newspapers sold than magazines?

Ⓐ Weekend 1

Ⓑ Weekend 2

Ⓒ Weekend 3

Ⓓ Weekend 4

4 About how many newspapers and magazines were sold during Weekend 3?

Ⓐ 35

Ⓑ 38

Ⓒ 45

Ⓓ 48

5 Which data does this line plot MOST LIKELY display?

```
        X
        X
        X   X   X
    X   X   X   X   X   X
    X   X   X   X   X   X
    X   X   X   X   X   X   X   X
    1   2   3   4   5   6   7   8
```

Ⓐ number of different school sports that students play in one weekend

Ⓑ number of words spelled incorrectly on a spelling test

Ⓒ number of years students have worn braces

Ⓓ number of cars owned by students' families

6 What data does this plot probably represent?

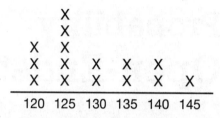

```
            X
            X
    X   X
    X   X   X   X   X
    X   X   X   X   X   X
    120 125 130 135 140 145
```

Ⓐ temperatures of the past 15 days

Ⓑ weights of the 15 wrestlers on a high-school team

Ⓒ number of minutes Sally was late for the last 15 trains at a train station

Ⓓ number of hours 15 students studied last week

Standard 6: Data Analysis and Probability
Open-Ended Questions

1.   In a spelling bee in Mr. Brown's class, students earned stars when they spelled words correctly. The chart shows how many stars the top 5 students earned.

Jason	12
Dylan	10
Laura	8
Melissa	8
Terence	6

Use this information to make a bar graph. Remember to label the horizontal and vertical axes and to give your graph a title.

2   Celia made a table of the number of words she misspelled in a monthly spelling tournament.

Month	Jan	Feb	Mar	Apr	May
Number of Words Misspelled	22	28	18	15	9

Draw a line plot that shows Celia's data.

3   A survey was taken of 100 students in the fifth grade at Burlington Elementary School to find out their favorite sports. These are the results of the survey.

Football: 25
Basketball: 35
Soccer: 10
Other: 30

Draw a graph that represents this information.

4   Cut out 8 small pieces of paper. Label the pieces of paper 1 though 8. Put the pieces in a paper bag, cup, or another container that you cannot see through. Pull out a piece of paper and record its number in a table. Replace the paper in the container. Repeat this process 40 times. Show your results in a bar graph.

Problem Solving

39 How to Solve Problems

4.7.8: Make precise calculations and check the validity of the results in the context of the problem.
4.7.10: Note the method of finding the solution and show a conceptual understanding of the method by solving similar problems.

When you solve a word problem, ask yourself what you have to do to get the answer. Do you need to add, subtract, multiply, or divide?

Example 1

Conrad took 45 baseball cards to a show. He bought 23 more. How can you find how many cards he has altogether?

STRATEGY: **Follow these steps.**

STEP 1: Read the problem carefully. What does it ask you to find?

The problem says, "how many cards he has altogether."

STEP 2: Decide what you have to do to find the number of cards.

"Altogether" is an important term to pay attention to.

SOLUTION: **You have to add: 45 + 23.**

Example 2

Tasha works as a computer specialist. She earns $25 per hour. She worked 8 hours last week. How can you find how much money she earned?

STRATEGY: **Do you need to add, subtract, multiply, or divide?**

STEP 1: Read the problem. What does the problem ask you to find?

You have to find how much Tasha earned last week. She worked 8 hours at $25 per hour.

STEP 2: What operation do you use?

SOLUTION: **You multiply since you know how much Tasha makes each hour and you know how many hours she worked. Multiply 25 × 8.**

Sometimes you have to use more than one operation.

Example 3

Megan gets paid $8 per hour as a dog walker. The first week in December, she worked 5 hours. The second week she worked 8 hours. The third week she worked 7 hours. The last week she worked 10 hours. How much money did she earn in December?

STRATEGY: **Follow the steps below.**

STEP 1: How can you figure out how much money she was paid?

You can multiply the number of hours she worked by the amount of money she is paid per hour.

STEP 2: Find the total number of hours she worked in December.

$5 + 8 + 7 + 10 = 30$

STEP 3: Multiply.

$30 \times 8 = 240$

SOLUTION: **Megan earned $240 in December.**

Example 4

Megan (from Example 3) worked from December through March last year. If she earned the same amount of money each month, how much did she earn altogether?

STRATEGY: **Do you need to add, subtract, multiply, or divide?**

You can either multiply or add. In this example, add.

December:	$240
January:	$240
February:	$240
March:	+ $240
All together	$960

SOLUTION: **Megan earned $960.**

Sample Test Questions

1 Doug walked 6.5 miles on Saturday and 2.3 miles on Sunday. How do you find how many more miles he walked on Saturday than on Sunday?

Ⓐ Add 6.5 and 2.3.

Ⓑ Subtract 2.3 from 6.5.

Ⓒ Multiply 6.5 by 2.3.

Ⓓ Divide 6.5 by 2.3.

2 Adrian has 27 dollars. He spends 15 dollars on a toy. How can you find out how much money he has left?

Ⓐ Subtract 15 from 27.

Ⓑ Add 15 and 27.

Ⓒ Multiply 15 by 27.

Ⓓ Divide 27 by 15.

3 A taxi costs 4 dollars for the first mile and 2 dollars for each mile after the first mile. How can you find the cost of a ride that is 11 miles?

Ⓐ Multiply 2 by 11.

Ⓑ Add 4 and 2, then multiply by 11.

Ⓒ Multiply 10 by 2, then add 4.

Ⓓ Subtract 2 from 4, then multiply by 11.

4 Annie needs to plant 40 flowers in 5 equal rows. How can you find out how many flowers are in each row?

Ⓐ Multiply 40 by 5.

Ⓑ Divide 40 by 5.

Ⓒ Add 40 and 5.

Ⓓ Subtract 5 from 40.

5   Stephen needs to figure out how to solve this problem.

> There are 9 baseball teams. 23 children can be on a team. How many children can play baseball altogether?

How can Stephen solve this problem? Be sure to include which mathematical operation and which numbers Stephen should use.

_____

_____

_____

_____

6   David needs to figure out how to solve this problem.

> There are 15 rows in a school auditorium. 25 students can sit in each row. How many students can sit in the auditorium altogether?

How can David solve this problem? Be sure to include which mathematical operation and which numbers David should use.

_____

_____

_____

_____

40 Strategies for Problem Solving

4.7.3: Apply strategies and results from simpler problems to solve more complex problems.
4.7.4: Use a variety of methods, such as words, numbers, symbols, charts, graphs, tables, diagrams, tools, and models to solve problems, justify arguments, and make conjectures.

You should know these strategies for solving problems.

Strategies

1. Act it out
2. Make a model
3. Draw a picture
4. Make a chart or graph
5. Look for a pattern
6. Make a simpler problem
7. Use logic
8. Work backward
9. Guess and check
10. Break the problem into parts

Example 1

Justin looked at his digital watch. The time was 1:23. The digits are consecutive. How many times does that happen each day?

STRATEGY: **Make a list.**

STEP 1: Write the times between noon and 1 p.m. that show digits in a row. There is one time: 12:34.

STEP 2: Write the times between 1:00 and 2:00 that show digits in a row. There is one time: 1:23.

STEP 3: Write the times for every hour after 2:00 until 12:00.

2:34, 3:45, 4:56

STEP 5: Count all the times listed above, and double the number because each time occurs twice in a 24-hour period.

SOLUTION: **Times with consecutive digits happen 10 times a day.**

Example 2

Jackie scored 4 points in her first basketball game. She scored 9 points in her second game, 14 points in her third game, and 19 points in her fourth game.

Game 1:   4 points

Game 2:   9 points

Game 3:   14 points

Game 4:   19 points

If this pattern continues, how many points will she score in her ninth game?

STRATEGY: **Find the pattern.**

STEP 1:   Find the difference between Game 2 and Game 1.

$9 - 4 = 5$

STEP 2:   Find the difference between Game 3 and Game 2.

$14 - 9 = 5$

STEP 3:   Find the difference between Game 4 and Game 3.

$19 - 14 = 5$

STEP 4:   What is the pattern?

Each game she scores 5 points more than the last game. The pattern is to add 5.

STEP 5:   Use the pattern to figure out how many points she will score in Game 9.

Game 5 = $19 + 15 = 24$

Game 6 = $24 + 5 = 29$

Game 7 = $29 + 5 = 34$

Game 8 = $34 + 5 = 39$

Game 9 = $39 + 5 = 44$

SOLUTION: **If the pattern continues, she will score 44 points in her ninth game.**

Sample Test Questions

1 Jeff lives 3 miles from Sarah. Sarah lives 4 miles from Rick. What is the shortest distance possible from Jeff's house to Rick's house?

Ⓐ 1 mile

Ⓑ 6 miles

Ⓒ 7 miles

Ⓓ 8 miles

2 A number is greater than 90 and less than 100. The tens digit of the number is 6 greater than the ones digit. What is the number?

Ⓐ 92

Ⓑ 93

Ⓒ 94

Ⓓ 97

3 If you switch the places of 2 numbers, the 3 sentences will all have the same answer.

$$9 + 3 = \boxed{}$$

$$5 + 8 = \boxed{}$$

$$4 + 7 = \boxed{}$$

Which 2 numbers could be switched?

Ⓐ 9 and 8

Ⓑ 5 and 7

Ⓒ 8 and 7

Ⓓ 8 and 4

4 How many diagonals are there in a regular hexagon? (A diagonal is a segment that connects two vertices and is not a side.)

Ⓐ 7

Ⓑ 8

Ⓒ 9

Ⓓ 10

5 Tim looked at his watch. The time was 10:00. This time shows 3 digits repeated in a row. How many times each day does the time repeat the same digit at least three times in a row? (Include 10:00 and use a 24-hour period.)

Ⓐ 32

Ⓑ 34

Ⓒ 36

Ⓓ 40

6 One way to arrange the three digits 1, 2, and 3 is in order 1-2-3. Another way is 3-2-1. How many different ways can these digits be arranged? (Count the two already shown.)

Ⓐ 4

Ⓑ 5

Ⓒ 6

Ⓓ 7

7 Quincy has a ribbon that is 10 inches long. She wants to cut the ribbon into 2 pieces so that one of the pieces is about twice as long as the other. At what point should she cut the piece?

Ⓐ between 5 and 6 inches

Ⓑ between 6 and 7 inches

Ⓒ between 7 and 8 inches

Ⓓ between 8 and 9 inches

8 Diane needs to solve the following problem.

Frances is conducting a science experiment on a plant. She measures the height of the plant each week. These are the measurements she has collected so far.

Week 1:	2 cm
Week 2:	4 cm
Week 3:	8 cm
Week 4:	16 cm

How tall will the plant probably be in Week 7?

Choose a strategy that can be used to solve this problem. Then solve the problem.

STRATEGY:

_____

_____

SOLUTION:

_____

_____

222

41 Missing Information

4.7.1: Analyze problems by identifying relationships, telling relevant from irrelevant information, sequencing and prioritizing information, and observing patterns.

Sometimes you need to identify what infomation is missing from a problem in order to solve it.

Example 1

Yesenia bought a dress that cost $38.50. How much change did she get?

What other information do you need to solve the problem?

STRATEGY: **Review the problem as if you were solving it.**

> **STEP 1:** What does the problem ask you to find?
>
> It asks you to find the amount of change Yesenia received.
>
> **STEP 2:** What information do you know?
>
> You know how much the dress cost.
>
> **STEP 3:** What information is missing?

SOLUTION: **The missing information is the amount of money Yesenia handed to the salesperson. For example, if she gave the salesperson $50, the change would be $11.50. If she gave the salesperson $40, the change would be $1.50.**

Example 2

Brendan divided his sports books equally into 3 piles. Can you calculate how many books were in each pile?

STRATEGY: **Figure out what the problem is asking. Then determine whether there is enough information to solve the problem.**

STEP 1: The problem is asking how many books Brendan put in each of 3 piles.

STEP 2: Decide what information the problem gives.

Brendan divided his books equally.

Brendan divided the books into 3 piles.

STEP 3: In order to calculate how many books Brendan put in each pile, you need to know how many books he began with.

SOLUTION: **This problem cannot be solved because information is missing.**

Example 3

Vanessa walks her neighbor's dog every morning at 7:00 A.M. She charges $9 per hour. How much money did she make last week?

Is there enough information to solve this problem? Explain.

STRATEGY: **Read the problem as if you were solving it.**

STEP 1: What does the problem ask you to find?

How much money Vanessa made last week

STEP 2: What information do you have?

Vanessa walks the dog every day at 7:00 A.M.

She charges $9 per hour.

STEP 3: Is any information missing?

Yes, the number of hours she walked the dog.

SOLUTION: **There is not enough information to solve this problem, since you do not know the number of hours she worked.**

Sample Test Questions

1 Lillian traveled 3 hours on a bus to visit a friend. What other information do you need to know if you want to find the time she got there?

(A) time she spent with her friend

(B) time she left on her trip

(C) time she came home

(D) name of the town she visited

2 Russell scored a total of 128 points for his basketball team this season. To find out if this was more than he scored last season, what other information do you need to know?

(A) number of points Russell scored last season

(B) number of points the team scored the season before

(C) number of points the team scored this season

(D) number of points his teammates scored

For Questions 3–5, decide whether or not there is enough information given to solve the problem. If there is not enough information, choose the answer that tells what information is needed.

3 Lee took $75 from his savings account to buy a bicycle. How much money is left in Lee's bank account?

(A) Enough information is given.

(B) Not enough information is given. You need to know how much the bicycle cost.

(C) Not enough information is given. You need to know how much money Lee put in his account last month.

(D) Not enough information is given. You need to know how much money was in the account before Lee bought the bicycle.

4 Janet bought 6 cookbooks. Each book cost $15. How much money did Janet spend on the books?

(A) Enough information is given.

(B) Not enough information is given. You need to know how much change Janet got when she paid for the books.

(C) Not enough information is given. You need to know the cost of the last cookbook Janet bought.

(D) Not enough information is given. You need to know how often Janet buys cookbooks.

5   Jack slept 15 hours on the first day of his vacation. How long did Jack sleep during his vacation?

Ⓐ Enough information is given.

Ⓑ Not enough information is given. You need to know how long Jack slept on the second day of his vacation.

Ⓒ Not enough information is given. You need to know how long Jack slept on the last day of his vacation.

Ⓓ Not enough information is given. You need to know how long Jack slept each day of his vacation.

6   Nancy danced for 2 hours without stopping. She rested for a half hour. Then she danced again.

What other information do you need to know to find how long she danced altogether?

Ⓐ time she stopped dancing

Ⓑ time she started dancing again

Ⓒ amount of time she danced the second time

Ⓓ time she first started dancing

7   Yasir paid $147 for several computer game programs. All the programs were the same price. What else do you need to know to find the cost of one program?

Ⓐ name of the store where he bought the programs

Ⓑ time it takes to finish each program

Ⓒ number of programs he bought

Ⓓ time of day he bought the programs

8   Monica needs to solve this problem.

Nicole drove 250 miles each day on her vacation. How many miles did she drive altogether?

Is there enough information to solve this problem?

_____

If yes, solve the problem.

If not, what information is needed in order to solve this problem?

_____

_____

_____

42 Different Ways to Solve Problems

4.7.2: Decide when and how to break a problem into simpler parts.
4.7.5: Express solutions clearly and logically by using the appropriate mathematical terms and notation. Support solutions with evidence in both verbal and symbolic work.

You can solve some problems more than one way. And some problems have more than one solution.

Example 1

A fence borders the four sides of a rectangular garden. The garden is 30 feet long and 20 feet wide. What is the total length of the fence?

Here are two ways to solve this problem.

STRATEGY 1: **Use the formula for perimeter.**

STEP 1: Write the formula for perimeter.

$P = 2 \times L + 2 \times W$

L stands for length, W stands for width

STEP 2: Substitute the actual length and width for L and W.

$P = 2 \times 30 + 2 \times 20 = 100$ feet

SOLUTION: **The length of the fence is 100 feet.**

STRATEGY 2:   **Draw a diagram.**

Perimeter is the distance around a figure.

The rectangle has two sides of 30 feet and two sides of 20 feet.

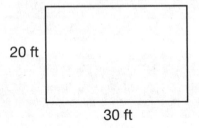

Add. 30 + 30 + 20 + 20 = 100 feet

SOLUTION: **The length of the fence is 100 feet.**

You can solve the problem of Example 1 in at least these two ways.

Sometimes a problem has more than one solution.

Example 2

At Jenn's school there is a weekly drawing for a prize. Each student writes a number from 1 to 500 on a card and places it in a box. One number is drawn and announced each Friday morning. Last Friday, the announcer said that the winning number was an even number between 70 and 80. What number did he announce?

STRATEGY: **Find the even numbers between 70 and 80.**

The even numbers between 70 and 80 are 72, 74, 76, and 78.

SOLUTION: **The number was 72, 74, 76, or 78.**

Sample Test Questions

1 Write one way to solve this problem. It is not necessary to find the answer.

Benjamin coaches a basketball team. He bought 3 basketballs for the team. Each ball cost $23.75. How much did all three balls cost?

_____

Write another way to solve this problem.

_____

_____

2 Write one way to solve this problem. It is not necessary to find the answer.

Find the area of this region.

_____

Write another way to solve this problem.

_____

_____

3 Elana planted 17 rows of tulips with 8 flowers in each row. How many tulips did she plant altogether?

Write one way to solve this problem.

_____

Write another way to solve this problem.

_____

_____

4 Jami's class had a jar of jellybeans. The class had to guess how many jellybeans were in the jar. The teacher said that the number of jellybeans was an odd number between 100 and 110. How many jellybeans were in the jar?

How many possible answers are there?

_____

Write down all the possible answers.

_____

_____

_____

5 Henry asked his friends to guess how many pieces of gum he was holding behind his back. He told them that the number of pieces of gum was an even number between 10 and 20.

How many possible answers are there?

_____

Write down all the possible answers.

_____

_____

6 Can you make change of 50 cents using exactly 9 coins? Explain.

_____

_____

_____

43 Solving Problems With Number Sentences

4.7.5: Express solutions clearly and logically by using the appropriate mathematical terms and notation. Support solutions with evidence in both verbal and symbolic work.

Sometimes, you have to pick a number sentence that can be used to solve a problem.

Example 1

Connie spent $8 in the morning and $7 in the afternoon. Which number sentence shows how much she spent all together?

Ⓐ $8 + 7 = \boxed{}$

Ⓑ $8 - 7 = \boxed{}$

Ⓒ $8 \times 7 = \boxed{}$

Ⓓ $8 + 8 = \boxed{}$

STRATEGY: **Look for key words in the problem.**

           STEP 1:   Find the key words in the question.

                       The key words are "all together."

           STEP 2:   What is the meaning of "all together"?

                       "All together" means that you should add.

SOLUTION: **The answer is A.**

Example 2

There are 4 teams in a basketball tournament. Each team has 8 students. Which number sentence shows how many students are on the 4 teams?

Ⓐ $8 \times 8 = \boxed{}$

Ⓑ $8 + 4 = \boxed{}$

Ⓒ $4 \times 8 = \boxed{}$

Ⓓ $4 \times 4 = \boxed{}$

STRATEGY: **Look for words that tell you what operation to use.**

STEP 1: What operation do you use—addition, subtraction, multiplication, or division?

Think: 4 teams of 8 students.

The fastest way to get the answer is to multiply.

STEP 2: What do you multiply?

You multiply 4×8, which is the same as adding 8 four times.

(You can solve the problem by adding: $8 + 8 + 8 + 8$, but multiplying is quicker.)

SOLUTION: **The answer is C.**

Sample Test Questions

1 Sue bought 17 pencils. Each pencil cost 6 cents. Which number sentence can you use to find the total cost in cents?

Ⓐ $17 + 6 =$ ☐

Ⓑ $17 - 6 =$ ☐

Ⓒ $17 \times 6 =$ ☐

Ⓓ $6 + 6 =$ ☐

2 Melissa called 8 people on Saturday and 17 people on Sunday. Which number sentence shows how many more people she called on Sunday than Saturday?

Ⓐ $8 + 17 =$ ☐

Ⓑ $17 - 8 =$ ☐

Ⓒ $17 \times 8 =$ ☐

Ⓓ $17 + 17 =$ ☐

3 At the Fun Ride Festival, you pay $4 for the first ride, and $2 for each ride after that. Which of the following could be used to find the cost of 4 rides?

Ⓐ $4 + 3 + 2$

Ⓑ $3 + 2 + 2 + 3$

Ⓒ $4 + 2 + 2$

Ⓓ $4 + 2 + 2 + 2$

4 Luke has 30 cookies. He wants to share them equally among 6 friends. Which number sentence shows how many cookies each friend will get?

Ⓐ $30 + 6 =$ ☐

Ⓑ $30 - 6 =$ ☐

Ⓒ $30 \times 6 =$ ☐

Ⓓ $30 \div 6 =$ ☐

5 Lisa runs 12 miles each week. Write a number sentence to show how many miles she runs in 6 weeks.

_____

44 How to Find a Reasonable Answer

4.7.8: Make precise calculations and check the validity of the results in the context of the problem.
4.7.9: Decide whether a solution is reasonable in the context of the original situation.

Some problems ask you to name a reasonable range for the answer.

Example 1

At a toy store, the least expensive board game costs $5, and the most expensive board game costs $13. Leslie bought 4 different board games. What is a reasonable range for the cost for the 4 board games?

STRATEGY: **Find the greatest possible cost and the least possible cost.**

STEP 1: How many board games did she buy?
Leslie bought 4 board games.

STEP 2: What was the cost of the least expensive board game?
The least expensive board game was $5.

STEP 3: How much would she pay if all the board games cost $5?
$4 \times 5 = \$20$ This is the least amount Leslie could have paid.

STEP 4: What was the cost of the most expensive board game?
The most expensive board game was $13.

STEP 5: How much would she pay if all the board games cost $13?
$4 \times 13 = \$52$.

SOLUTION: **A reasonable range for the amount Leslie spent is between $20 and $52.**

234

Example 2

Matthew swims an hour each day. He swims 30 to 50 laps each hour. What is a reasonable range for the number of laps he swims in a week?

STRATEGY: **Find the least possible number of laps he swims and the greatest possible number of laps he swims.**

        STEP 1:   Find the least number of laps he could swim.

                    The least number of laps he swims in one hour is 30. So, the least number of laps in a week (7 days) is 210.

        STEP 2:   Find the greatest number of laps he could swim.

                    The greatest number of laps he swims in one hour is 50. So, the greatest number of laps in 7 days is 350.

SOLUTION: **Matthew swims between 210 and 350 laps in one week.**

Sample Test Questions

1 George eats from 6 to 12 eggs in a week. What is a reasonable range for the number of eggs George eats in 7 weeks?

Ⓐ less than 42 eggs

Ⓑ 42 to 84 eggs

Ⓒ 42 to 90 eggs

Ⓓ 42 to 100 eggs

2 Lisa plays tennis every week. The least amount she plays is 4 hours a week. The greatest amount she plays is 11 hours. Which is a reasonable number of hours she could play in 9 weeks?

Ⓐ 110 hours

Ⓑ 90 hours

Ⓒ 30 hours

Ⓓ 10 hours

3 Manny earns $100 each day he works. If he works between 10 and 20 days a month, which is a reasonable amount he could earn in a month?

Ⓐ $500

Ⓑ $1,500

Ⓒ $2,200

Ⓓ $2,500

4 Nora watches 2 to 4 hours of TV each day. Which is a reasonable amount of time she could spend watching TV in a week?

Ⓐ 7 hours

Ⓑ 10 hours

Ⓒ 20 hours

Ⓓ 30 hours

5 Clement reads 3 to 4 books a month. Which is a reasonable number of books he could read in a year?

Ⓐ 15 books   Ⓒ 45 books

Ⓑ 30 books   Ⓓ 60 books

6 Each book in a series has 50 to 100 pages each. If Krista reads 3 of the books each week, which is a reasonable number of pages she could read in a week?

Ⓐ 120   Ⓒ 200

Ⓑ 150   Ⓓ 300

7 Sheila writes 4 to 8 stories each week. Show how to find a reasonable number of stories she could write in 6 weeks.

_____

_____

_____

236

Progress Check for Lessons 39–44

1 Samantha spent $25.46 at the mall. She started with $40. Which number sentence shows how much money she had left?

Ⓐ 25.46 + 40 = ☐

Ⓑ 25.46 − 40 = ☐

Ⓒ 40 − 25.46 = ☐

Ⓓ 40 × 25.46 = ☐

2 Dorothy earns $6.25 each hour she works at Columbia Computers Company. Don earns $7.50 each hour he works for the same company. If Don works 6 hours a day and Dorothy 7 hours a day, who earns more each day? How much more?

Ⓐ Dorothy earns $1.75 more.

Ⓑ Dorothy earns $1.25 more.

Ⓒ Don earns $1.75 more.

Ⓓ Don earns $1.25 more.

3 Smith has 18 dollars and Caroline has 20 dollars. How many nickels would that be altogether? Which number sentence could be used to solve this problem?

Ⓐ (18 + 20) × 100 = ☐

Ⓑ (18 + 20) × 20 = ☐

Ⓒ (18 + 20) × 10 = ☐

Ⓓ (18 × 20) + 20 = ☐

4 Carlos scored 3 points in the first basketball game, 7 points in the second sgame, and 11 points in the third game. If this pattern continues, how many points will Carlos score in the fifth game?

Ⓐ 15

Ⓑ 17

Ⓒ 19

Ⓓ 21

5 Penney says she can type 73 words per minute. At that rate, about how many words can she type in a half hour?

Ⓐ 1,500 words

Ⓑ 1,700 words

Ⓒ 2,100 words

Ⓓ 5,000 words

6 Jimmy said he took 5 steps forward and 3 steps backward each minute for 20 minutes. How far did he get?

Ⓐ 10 steps backward

Ⓑ 10 steps forward

Ⓒ 20 steps forward

Ⓓ 40 steps forward

7 Last Tuesday, 46 children went on a field trip to the art museum and 68 children went on a field trip to the planetarium. How many more children went to the planetarium than to the art museum?

Ⓐ 11 children

Ⓑ 21 children

Ⓒ 22 children

Ⓓ 26 children

8 Dawn is 10 years old. Her brother is 14 years old. Her uncle is 26 years older than she is. How old is her uncle?

Ⓐ 27 years

Ⓑ 36 years

Ⓒ 37 years

Ⓓ 43 years

Standard 7: Problem Solving
Open-Ended Questions

1 What information is missing from this problem?

Max and Billie mowed lawns for 12 hours last week. They decided to split the money they made evenly. How much did each boy make?

Supply the missing information in this problem and then solve the problem. Show your work.

_____

2 Write a number sentence to solve this problem.

Jamie rented two videos for $8 and then spent another $6 on a plant for her mother. How much did she spend altogether?

_____

3 Five students lined up for gym. Ryan was in front of Jenny. Jenny was in front of Magda. Julio was behind Celia. Celia was first in line. In what order were the students lined up?

What strategy can you use to solve this problem?

_____

4 Tim has 78 balloons. He would like to give an equal number of balloons to each of his 6 friends. How many balloons will each friend get?

_____

5 Willa baked cookies for her birthday party. She put 12 cookies on a cookie sheet. She baked 3 sheets of cookies. How many cookies does Willa bake altogether?

_____

6 Barbara rides her bike 15 to 35 miles a week. Show how to find a reasonable range for the number of miles she rides her bike in 7 weeks.

_____

Take-Home Math Activities

Anna & Zeke's
Table of Contents

For the Student:

The Take-Home Math Activities contains mathematical terms, definitions, and examples in alphabetical order. Each page will contain at least one **Do I Understand?** question for you to determine if you understand a key idea. At the end of the book there is a Glossary, a Facts Practice, a list of abbreviations, measures of time, math symbols, and formulas.

From,

Anna & Zeke

Addition

An operation on two or more numbers to find a sum.

● Parts of Addition

These are the parts of an addition problem.

$$
\begin{array}{r}
45 \\
+ \ 32 \\
\hline
77
\end{array}
\begin{array}{l}
\longleftarrow \textbf{addend} \\
\longleftarrow \textbf{addend} \\
\longleftarrow \textbf{sum}
\end{array}
$$

● Add Whole Numbers

To add whole numbers, add the digits from right to left. **Regroup** if necessary.

$$
\begin{array}{r}
11 \\
537 \\
+ \ 394 \\
\hline
931
\end{array}
$$

● Add Money

Money amounts are also added from right to left.

Remember to include the dollar sign ($) and place the decimal point in the sum.

$$
\begin{array}{r}
1 \quad\ 1 \\
\$465.37 \\
+ \ 192.43 \\
\hline
\$657.80
\end{array}
$$

● Add Decimals

Adding decimals is like adding money. There may be a different number of places after the decimal. Align the digits on the decimal point. If necessary, insert a zero at the end of the decimal.

$$
\begin{array}{r}
11 \\
42.7\mathbf{0} \\
+ \ 38.95 \\
\hline
81.65
\end{array}
$$

● Add Fractions with Like Denominators

To add fractions with **like denominators** add the numerators. The denominator remains the same. Write the sum in simplest form if possible.

$$\frac{3}{12} + \frac{5}{12} = \frac{5+3}{12} = \frac{8}{12} = \frac{2}{3}$$

● Add Fractions with Unlike Denominators

To add fractions with unlike denominators, follow these steps:

Write equivalent fractions using the LCD.

$$
\begin{array}{r}
\frac{1}{6} = \quad \frac{1}{6} \\
+ \ \frac{1}{3} = + \frac{2}{6} \\
\hline
\end{array}
$$

Add the numerators. Simplify if possible.

$$
\begin{array}{r}
\frac{1}{6} \\
+ \ \frac{2}{6} \\
\hline
\frac{3}{6} = \frac{1}{2}
\end{array}
$$

Algebra

A type of math that uses variables as a way to solve a problem.

● Variables

A **variable** is a symbol that represents a number. Usually a variable will be a letter, but it can also be a □.

● Equations

An **equation** is a number sentence with an equal sign (=). Examples of equations are $3 + 4 = 7$ and $2 + x = 6$.

● Expressions

An **expression** is a group of numbers and symbols that shows a mathematical quantity. For example, if your mother is 27 years older than you are, your mother's age can be represented as $a + 27$, when a represents your age.

● Solve Addition and Subtraction Equations

Addition and subtraction are **inverse operations**.

Find the value of x in $8 + x = 24$.
Subtract to find x.
$24 - 8 = x$ $24 - 8 = 16$
$x = 16$

Find the value of y in $y - 12 = 19$.
Add to find y.
$19 + 12 = y$ $19 + 12 = 31$
$y = 31$

● Solve Multiplication and Division Equations

Multiplication and division are inverse operations.

Find the value of b in $4b = 24$.
Divide to find b.
$24 \div 4 = b$ $24 \div 4 = 6$
$b = 6$

Find the value of c in $c \div 3 = 7$.
Multiply to find c.
$7 \times 3 = c$ $7 \times 3 = 21$
$c = 21$

● Functions

A **function** is a relationship in which one quantity depends on another quantity. A function has a rule that must be followed for every set of values.

This function table shows the relationship between the number of days and the number of weeks.

weeks (w)	1	2	3	4
days (d)	7	14	21	28

The function shows that $w = 7d$.

Do I Understand?

1. What is the value of n in $5 + n = 13$? _____

2.

x	1	2	3	4
y	3	5		9

What is the missing number in this function table? _____

4

Angles

An angle is formed when two rays or line segments meet at the same endpoint.

● Parts of an Angle

An **angle** can be named in three ways. The letter for the vertex is always in the middle.

This angle can be named ∠ABC, ∠CBA, or ∠B.

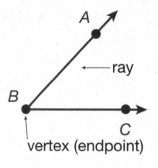

ray

vertex (endpoint)

● Classification of Angles

There are four types of angles. Angles are measured in **degrees (°)**.

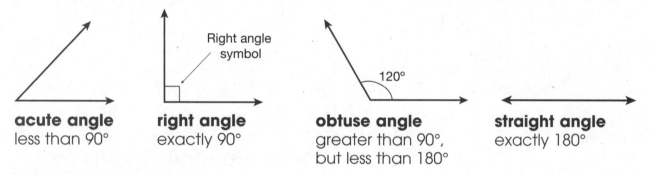

Right angle symbol

120°

acute angle
less than 90°

right angle
exactly 90°

obtuse angle
greater than 90°, but less than 180°

straight angle
exactly 180°

● Measure Angles

A **protractor** is used to measure angles. To use a protractor, align the center of the protractor with the vertex of the angle.

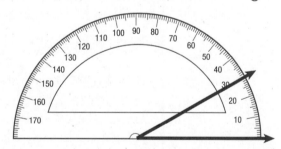

This angle measures 30°.

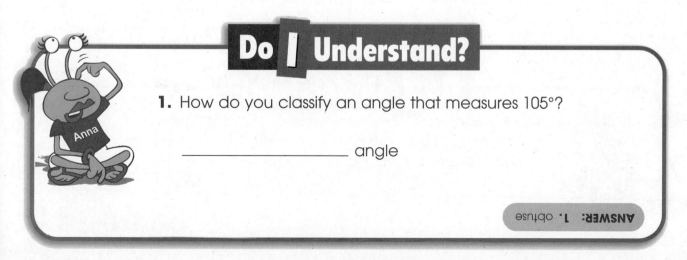

Do I Understand?

1. How do you classify an angle that measures 105°?

_____ angle

5

Area
The number of square units needed to cover a region

● Square Units

Area is expressed in **square units (or units²)**. A square unit is a square, one of whose sides is a given unit of length. Square units can be in inches, feet, centimeters, meters, or other units.

An example of how square units work is in this grid.

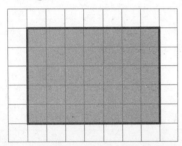

Count the total number of square units that are shaded. The area of the shaded part is 35 square units.

● Area of a Rectangle

To find the area of a rectangle, use a formula.

Area = length × width
$A = l \times w$
Find the area of the figure below.

7 cm

3 cm

$A = 7 \text{ cm} \times 3 \text{ cm} = 21 \text{ cm}^2$
The area of the rectangle is 21 cm².

● Area of a Square

A square has 4 equal sides. To find the area of a square, multiply the length of one of the sides by itself.

The formula for the area of a square is Area = side × side. $A = s^2$
Find the area of this square.

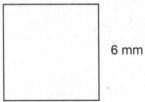

6 mm

6 mm

$A = 6 \text{ mm} \times 6 \text{ mm} = 36 \text{ mm}^2$
The area of the square is 36 mm².

● Compound Figures

A compound figure can be broken into two smaller figures in order to find the area.

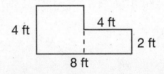

4 ft   4 ft

2 ft

8 ft

Break the figure into a square and a rectangle. The square measures 4 feet by 4 feet and the rectangle measures 4 feet by 2 feet. Find the area of each then add the areas.

Square: 4 ft × 4 ft = 16 ft²
Rectangle: 4 ft × 2 ft = 8 ft²
Add the areas: 16 ft² + 8 ft² = 24 ft².

Do I Understand?

Zeke

1. A rectangle has a length of 8 inches and a width of 4 inches. What is the area of the rectangle?

_____ in.²

Average
The sum of a set of numbers divided by the number of addends

● Averages in the Real World

Examples of **average** include miles **per** hour, cost per unit, points per game, and population density. There are many other ways averages can be used, such as determining your grades.

● Find the Mean

An average, or **mean**, is found by finding the sum of a **data** set and then dividing the sum by the number of addends. For example, the table shows the number of books taken out from the school library last week.

Monday	Tuesday	Wednesday	Thursday	Friday
15	20	18	17	15

Add the numbers.
$$15 + 20 + 18 + 17 + 15 = 85$$

Divide the sum by the number of addends.
$$85 \div 5 = 17$$

The mean is 17.

● Find the Range

The **range** is the difference between the greatest number and the least number in a data set. To find the range of the data set above, subtract $20 - 15 = 5$. The range is 5.

● Find the Median

The **median** is the middle number of a data set when the numbers are ordered.

Order the numbers from least to greatest.

15, 15, **17**, 18, 20

The middle number is 17, so the median is 17.

If there is an even number of data, find the mean of the two middle numbers.

For example, in the set 3, 4, 5, 7, 8, 9, the two middle numbers are 5 and 7. To find the mean of the two middle numbers, find the sum of $5 + 7 = 12$ and divide by 2: $12 \div 2 = 6$. The median is 6.

● Find the Mode

The **mode** is the number that occurs most often in a data set.

Use this data set to find the mode.

27, 35, 43, 35, 19, 27, 35

The number 35 occurs most often, so it is the mode.

Do I Understand?

Use this data set, 56, 48, 52, 48, 51, to find the following:

1. mean   **2.** range   **3.** median   **4.** mode

_____   _____   _____   _____

ANSWERS: 1. 51   2. 8   3. 51   4. 48

7

Circles

A plane figure having all points the same distance from a fixed point called the center.

● Parts of a Circle

Here are the parts of a **circle**.

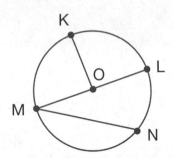

All points of the circle are the same distance from the **center**. Point O is the center. A circle is named by its center.

A **radius** is a line segment from the center of the circle to any point on the circle. Line segments $\overline{OK}$, $\overline{OL}$, and $\overline{OM}$ are the radii of circle O.

A **chord** is a line segment from one point of a circle to another point. Line segments $\overline{LM}$ and $\overline{MN}$ are chords.

A **diameter** is a chord that passes through the center of the circle. Line segment $\overline{LM}$ is a diameter of circle O.

Compare and Order

To determine whether a number is greater than, less than, or equal to another number.

● What the Symbols Mean

> is greater than
< is less than
= is equal to

● Compare Whole Numbers

Compare the digits from left to right.

$$4{,}223 \bigcirc 4{,}261$$

The thousands and hundreds digits are the same in both numbers.

Compare the tens.
4,2**2**3   2 < 6 so
4,2**6**1   4,223 < 4,261

● Compare Decimals

To compare decimals, align the numbers on the decimal point.

$$5.3 \bigcirc 5.19$$

The ones digits are the same.

Compare the tenths.
5.**3**   3 > 1, so
5.**1**9   5.3 > 5.19

Do I Understand?

1. How can you classify $\overline{AB}$?

_____

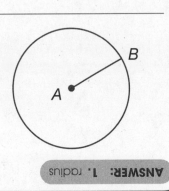

Do I Understand?

Compare.
Use >, <, or =.

1. 68.27 $\bigcirc$ 8.925

● Order Numbers

Numbers can be ordered from least to greatest or from greatest to least.

Order the following numbers from least to greatest:

465, 382, 493

Hundreds	Tens	Ones
4	6	5
3	8	2
4	9	3

Order the digits from left to right.

Since $3 < 4$, 382 is the least number.

Compare 465 and 493.

Since $6 < 9$, $465 < 493$.

The order from least to greatest is 382, 465, and 493.

● Compare Fractions with Like Denominators

Fractions with like denominators can be compared by their numerators. The greater the numerator, the greater the fraction.

For example, $\frac{1}{4} < \frac{3}{4}$.

● Compare Fractions with Like Numerators

Fractions with like numerators can be compared by their denominators. The greater the denominator, the less value the fraction has.

For example, $\frac{1}{4} < \frac{1}{3}$.

● Compare Fractions with Unlike Denominators

To compare fractions with unlike denominators, it is necessary to find equivalent fractions.
Compare $\frac{5}{6}$ and $\frac{3}{4}$.

First, find the **least common denominator (LCD)** of $\frac{5}{6}$ and $\frac{3}{4}$. The LCD is the least common multiple (LCM) of the denominators.

Multiples of 6: 6, 12, 18, 24. . .
Multiples of 4: 4, 8, 12, 16, 20. . .

So, 12 is the LCD of $\frac{5}{6}$ and $\frac{3}{4}$.

Write equivalent fractions for $\frac{5}{6}$ and $\frac{3}{4}$ with 12 as a denominator.

$$\frac{5}{6} \times \frac{2}{2} = \frac{10}{12} \qquad \frac{3}{4} \times \frac{3}{3} = \frac{9}{12}$$

Compare $\frac{10}{12}$ and $\frac{9}{12}$ by comparing the numerators.

$$\frac{10}{12} > \frac{9}{12}, \text{ so } \frac{5}{6} > \frac{3}{4}.$$

Do I Understand?

Compare each pair of fractions. Use >, <, or =.

2. $\frac{5}{8} \bigcirc \frac{3}{8}$

3. $\frac{2}{5} \bigcirc \frac{2}{3}$

4. $\frac{1}{4} \bigcirc \frac{2}{8}$

ANSWERS: 1. < 2. > 3. =

9

Congruent and Similar Figures

CONGRUENT FIGURES - Two figures that have the same shape and size.
SIMILAR FIGURES - Two figures that have the same shape but may have different sizes.

● Congruent Figures

Congruent figures have the same shape and size. Below are examples of congruent figures.

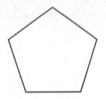 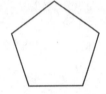

The pentagons are congruent.

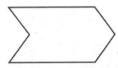 

The hexagons are congruent.

● Similar Figures

Similar figures have the same shape but may have different sizes. Congruent figures are always similar. Below are examples of similar figures that are not congruent.

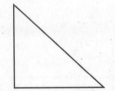

The right triangles are similar but not congruent.

The squares are similar but not congruent.

● Figures That are Always Similar

A **regular polygon** is a polygon with all equal sides and equal angles. Regular polygons are always similar to each other because they always have the same shape.

An equilateral triangle and a square are examples of regular polygons.

Do I Understand?

1. Are the following figures congruent, similar but not congruent, or neither?

_____

10

Decimals

A number with at least one digit to the right of a decimal point.

● Place Value

A **decimal** is a number with a **decimal point (.)**. A decimal point separates the whole number from the part that represents part of one whole. The place-value chart shows the names of each of the places.

Ones	.	Tenths	Hundredths	Thousandths

The decimal 3.8 is made up of 3 ones and 8 **tenths**.

The decimal 0.279 is made up of 2 tenths, 7 **hundredths**, and 9 **thousandths**.

● Read Decimals

To read the decimal 9.315, follow these steps:

Read the whole-number part first. The word *and* separates the whole-number part from the decimal part.

nine and

Read the number part of the decimal.

three hundred fifteen

Read the place of the decimal.

thousandths

So, 9.315 is read nine and three hundred fifteen thousandths.

● Change Decimals to Fractions

Change 0.4 into a fraction.

To change a decimal into a fraction, follow these steps:

Write the decimal as the numerator with its place as the denominator:

$$\frac{4}{10}$$

Simplify the fraction.

$$\frac{4}{10} \div \frac{2}{2} = \frac{2}{5}$$

● Change Fractions to Decimals

Change $\frac{3}{5}$ to a decimal.

To change a fraction to a decimal, divide the numerator by the denominator. The quotient is a decimal.

$$3 \div 5 = 0.6$$

Do I Understand?

1. What is five and two hundred thirty-nine thousandths written as a decimal?

_____

2. What is $\frac{3}{4}$ written as a decimal? _____

11

Division

An operation on two numbers that tells how many groups or how many in each group.

● How to Write a Division Problem

There are two ways to write a **division** problem.

$$42 \div 7 = 6$$

$$\begin{array}{r} 6 \\ 7\overline{)42} \\ -42 \\ \hline 0 \end{array}$$

These are the parts of a division problem.

$$\begin{array}{r} \text{quotient} \\ \text{divisor} \longrightarrow 7\overline{)42} \longleftarrow \text{dividend} \\ -42 \\ \hline 0 \end{array}$$

● Remainders

Division problems may have a **remainder**. A remainder is a number less than the divisor that remains after division is completed. For example:

$$\begin{array}{r} 4\ \text{R3} \longleftarrow \text{remainder} \\ 6\overline{)27} \\ -24 \\ \hline 3 \end{array}$$

The letter R stands for remainder. Since the remainder (3) is less than the divisor (6), the remainder is R3.

● Division by 1-Digit Divisors

Divide $592 \div 8$.

$$\begin{array}{r} 7 \\ 8\overline{)592} \\ -56 \\ \hline \end{array}$$

There are not enough hundreds to divide. There are enough tens to divide. Divide $59 \div 8$. Since $8 \times 7 = 56$, there are 7 tens.

$$\begin{array}{r} 7 \\ 8\overline{)592} \\ -56 \\ \hline 32 \end{array}$$

Subtract $59 - 56$. Bring down the 2 ones.

$$\begin{array}{r} 74 \\ 8\overline{)592} \\ -56 \\ \hline 32 \\ -32 \\ \hline 0 \end{array}$$

Divide $32 \div 8$. Since $8 \times 4 = 32$, there are 4 ones.

● Division by 2-Digit Divisors

Divide $123 \div 16$.

$$\begin{array}{r} 7\ \text{R11} \\ 16\overline{)123} \\ -112 \\ \hline 11 \end{array}$$

There are not enough tens to divide. Divide the ones. Multiply $16 \times 7 = 112$. Subtract $123 - 112 = 11$. The remainder is 11.

Do I Understand?

Divide.

1. $40 \div 8$ **2.** $7\overline{)53}$ **3.** $7\overline{)266}$ **4.** $24\overline{)397}$

Estimation

Finding an answer that is close to the exact answer.

● Estimate by Rounding

Sometimes it is not necessary to find an exact answer. An **estimate** may be all that is required. The most basic way to estimate is to **round** numbers. Rounding is to find the value of a number based on a given place value. There is more than one way to round.

What is 42,683 rounded to the nearest thousand?

To round a number to a given place, follow these rules:

Look at the digit to the right of the place you are rounding. When rounding to the nearest thousand, look at the hundreds place.

   42,**6**83

If the digit is less than 5, the digit in the place you are rounding remains the same. If the digit is 5 or greater, add 1 to the digit in the place you are rounding.

   Since 6 > 5, add 1 to the thousands place.

So, 42,683 rounds to 43,000 to the nearest thousand.

● Estimate Sums and Differences

To estimate a sum, round each addend to a given place. The same holds true for subtraction. The actual answers are given to the left of the estimated answers. See that the estimated answers are close to the actual answers.

$$
\begin{array}{rcr}
2{,}292 \rightarrow & 2{,}000 \\
+\ 4{,}738 \rightarrow & +\ 5{,}000 \\
\hline
7{,}030 & 7{,}000
\end{array}
\qquad
\begin{array}{rcr}
6{,}875 \rightarrow & 7{,}000 \\
-\ 3{,}605 \rightarrow & -\ 4{,}000 \\
\hline
3{,}270 & 3{,}000
\end{array}
$$

● Estimate Products and Quotients

To estimate a product, round the factor to a given place and multiply. For example, to estimate 387×19, round to $400 \times 20 = 8{,}000$.

So, 387×19 is about 8,000.

To estimate a quotient, it is necessary to use **compatible numbers**. Compatible numbers are numbers that are easy to divide mentally. For example, to estimate $675 \div 32$, you would not round the dividend to 680, you would use compatible numbers, which are 600 and 30. Since $600 \div 30 = 20$, $675 \div 32$ is about 20.

Do I Understand?

Estimate. Show your work.

1.   6,391
   + 5,828

2.   8,842
   − 2,121

3.   93
   × 52

4. 869 ÷ 22

Factors and Multiples

FACTOR - a number that is multiplied to get a product.
MULTIPLE - a number that is the product of a number and any whole number.

● Factors and Products

Numbers that are multiplied to get a product are called **factors**. A product must have at least two factors, although they may be the same number. Products that have the same factors are called **square numbers**.

7	×	5	=	35
factor		**factor**		**product**

8	×	8	=	64
factor		**factor**		**product**

● Factors of a Number

The factors of a number are those numbers in which it is possible to find a product.

For example, the factors of 36 are 1, 2, 3, 4, 6, 9, 12, 18, and 36 because 1 × 36, 2 × 18, 3 × 12, 4 × 9, and 6 × 6 all equal 36.

● Multiples of a Number

A **multiple** is a number that is the product of a number and any whole number.

For example, some of the multiples of 6 are 6, 12, 18, 24, 30, 36, 42, and so on.

● Greatest Common Factor (GCF)

The **greatest common factor (GCF)** of 2 or more numbers is the greatest whole number that is a common factor of the numbers. For example, find the GCF of 18 and 30.

1. List the factors of both numbers.
18: 1, 2, 3, 6, 9, 18
30: 1, 2, 3, 5, 6, 10, 15, 30
2. Find the common factors: 1, 2, 3, 6

The GCF of 18 and 30 is 6.

● Least Common Multiple (LCM)

The **least common multiple** of 2 or more numbers is the least whole number greater than 0 that is a multiple of each of the numbers. For example, find the LCM of 6 and 8.

1. Find the first multiples of 6:
6, 12, 18, 24, 30, . . .

2. Find the first multiples of 8:
8, 16, 24, . . .

The LCM of 6 and 8 is 24.

Do I Understand?

Zeke

1. What are the factors of 27?

2. What is the GCF of 12 and 15?

_____   _____

Fractions

A number that names part of a whole or a group.

● Parts of a Fraction

The **denominator**, or bottom number, tells how many equal parts there are in a **fraction**. The **numerator**, or top number, tells how many of those equal parts are being considered.

$$\frac{2}{5} \begin{array}{l} \longleftarrow \textbf{numerator} \\ \longleftarrow \textbf{denominator} \end{array}$$

● Use Fractions

A fraction can name parts of a whole.

The fraction $\frac{3}{8}$ represents the part of the rectangle that is shaded. The fraction $\frac{5}{8}$ represents the part that is not shaded.

A fraction can also name part of a group.

The fraction $\frac{7}{10}$ represents the white marbles. The fraction $\frac{3}{10}$ represents the black marbles.

● Equivalent Fractions

Equivalent fractions are two or more different fractions that name the same amount. To find an equivalent fraction, multiply or divide the numerator and denominator of the fraction by the same number.

For example, $\frac{3}{4}$ and $\frac{6}{8}$ are equivalent fractions since $\frac{3}{4} \times \frac{2}{2} = \frac{6}{8}$.

● Simplest Form

A fraction written in **simplest form** has 1 for the only number that evenly divides into both the numerator and denominator. For example, $\frac{3}{4}$ is written in simplest form because 1 is the only common factor of 3 and 4. The fraction $\frac{8}{10}$ is not in simplest form because 2 is a common factor of 8 and 10.

$$\frac{8}{10} \longrightarrow \frac{8 \div 2}{10 \div 2} = \frac{4}{5}$$

● Mixed Numbers

A **mixed number** is a number that has a whole-number part and a fraction part. An example of a mixed number is $2\frac{3}{4}$.

Do I Understand?

1. What is $\frac{6}{9}$ written in simplest form?

_____

ANSWER: 1. $\frac{2}{3}$

15

Graphs

A drawing that shows information.

● Pictographs

A **pictograph** uses a picture or symbol to compare information. A **key** tells how many items each symbol represents.

This pictograph shows how many CDs a record store sold each day for 4 days.

CD House: Sales for the Week of 8/12/04

Day	CDs Sold
Mon.	💿 💿 💿 💿 💿 ◗
Tues.	💿 💿 💿 💿
Wed.	💿 💿 💿 💿 💿 💿
Thurs.	💿 💿 💿 💿

Each 💿 = 20 CDs.

To read a pictograph, multiply the value of the key by the number of symbols. If there is a half symbol, take half the value of the key.

To find how many CDs were sold Monday, multiply 5 × 20 = 100. There is also half of a CD, which represents 10 CDs sold. Add 100 + 10 = 110 to find the total number of CDs sold Monday.

● Bar Graphs

A **bar graph** uses bars of different lengths to compare information. This bar graph shows the amount of money that a school store earned each school day.

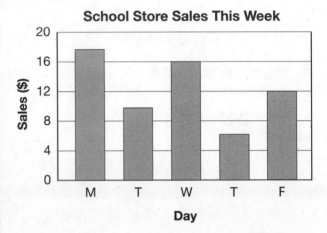

School Store Sales This Week

The days of the week are listed at the bottom of the graph. The number of dollars earned is shown on the left side of the graph. The dollars earned are in **intervals** of 4. Each number is 4 apart from the next number. If a bar falls between two numbers, it has the value half way between the two numbers that it falls between.

You can see that the store earned $18 Monday.

Do I Understand?

1. Use the pictograph. How many more CDs were sold on Wednesday than on Tuesday?

_____ CDs

2. Use the bar graph. How much money did the store earn on Thursday and Friday altogether?

$ _____

Graphs
(continued)

● Line Graphs

A **line graph** is read like a coordinate grid. Line graphs are used to show change over time. The points are connected by a line, which shows the change. This line graph shows the temperature each hour from 12:00 noon to 6:00.

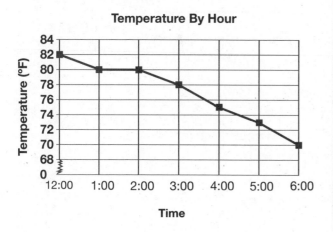

Temperature By Hour

To find the temperature at 3:00, find the point above 3:00. Then look to the left to find the value of the dot. At 3:00, the temperature was 78°F.

● Circle Graphs

A **circle graph** shows the parts of a whole. This circle graph shows the championships won by WNBA teams.

WNBA Championships

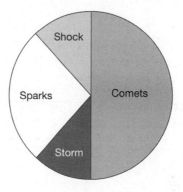

The larger the section of a circle graph, the greater its part of the whole. From reading the graph, it is easy to see that the Comets have won the most WNBA championships.

Do I Understand?

3. Use the line graph. What was the temperature at 1:00?

_____

4. Use the circle graph. What fraction represents the number of championships that the Comets have won?

_____

Lines

A straight path that goes in two directions without end.

● Lines

A **line** is a straight path that goes in two directions without end. This line can be read as either $\overleftrightarrow{AB}$ or $\overleftrightarrow{BA}$.

● Line Segments

A **line segment** is a part of a line that has two endpoints. This line segment can be named as either $\overline{MN}$ or $\overline{NM}$.

● Rays

A **ray** is part of a line that has one endpoint and goes in one direction without end. A ray is read with the endpoint first. This ray is read $\overrightarrow{YZ}$.

● Types of Lines

There are 3 types of pairs of lines.
Parallel lines never meet and remain the same distance apart.
Intersecting lines are lines that cross.
Perpendicular lines are lines that intersect at a right angle.

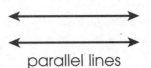

parallel lines

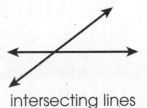

intersecting lines

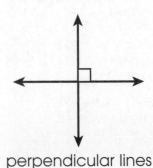

perpendicular lines

Do I Understand?

1. Name a straight path with one endpoint that goes forever in one direction.

_____

2. Which type of lines remain the same distance apart and never meet?

_____

18

Measurement

The measures of length, capacity, weight/mass in the customary and metric systems.

● Customary Measurement

The customary system of measure is used in the United States. Here are the most common customary units of measure.

Customary Units of Length		
1 **foot (ft)**	=	12 **inches (in.)**
1 **yard (yd)**	=	36 in. or 3 ft
1 **mile (mi)**	=	5,280 ft or 1,760 yd

Customary Units of Weight		
1 **pound (lb)**	=	16 **ounces (oz)**
1 **ton (T)**	=	2,000 lb

Customary Units of Capacity		
1 **cup (c)**	=	8 **fluid ounces (fl oz)**
1 **pint (pt)**	=	2c or 16 fl oz
1 **quart (qt)**	=	2pt or 32 fl oz
1 **gallon (gal)**	=	4 qt or 128 fl oz

The line segment below is 1 inch long.

A piece of paper is about 1 foot long. The width of a door is about 1 yard long. A mile is the distance that an adult can walk in about 20 minutes.

A small eraser weighs about 1 ounce. A basketball weighs about 1 pound. A small car weighs about 1 ton.

● Metric Measurement

The metric system is used in most of the world. The metric system is based on the number 10. When you change from one unit to another, you usually multiply or divide by 10.

Metric Units of Length	
1 **centimeter (cm)**	= 10 **millimeters (mm)**
1 **meter (m)**	= 100 cm or 1,000 mm
1 **kilometer (km)**	= 1,000 m

Metric Units of Mass	
1 **gram (g)**	= 1,000 **milligrams (mg)**
1 **kilogram (kg)**	= 1,000 g

Metric Units of Capacity	
1 **liter (L)**	= 1,000 **milliliters (mL)**

The line segment below is 1 centimeter long.

A meter is a little longer than a yard.

A kilometer is the distance that an adult can walk in about 10 minutes.

A hardcover book has a mass of about 1 kilogram.

A liter is a little larger than a quart.

Do I Understand?

1. If a person is 5 feet 4 inches tall, how tall is that person in inches?

_____ inches

2. How many meters are equal to 5 kilometers?

_____ meters

Multiplication

A shortcut for repeated addition.

● How to Write a Multiplication Problem

There are two ways to write a multiplication problem.

$$8 \times 7 = 56 \qquad \begin{array}{r} 7 \\ \times\ 8 \\ \hline 56 \end{array}$$

These are the parts of a multiplication problem.

multiplication   7 ← **factor**
sign → $\times$ 8 ← **factor**
      56 ← **product**

● Multiplication Table

A multiplication table shows the facts of multiplication.

×	0	1	2	3	4	5	6	7	8	9
0	0	0	0	0	0	0	0	0	0	0
1	0	1	2	3	4	5	6	7	8	9
2	0	2	4	6	8	10	12	14	16	18
3	0	3	6	9	12	15	18	21	24	27
4	0	4	8	12	16	20	24	28	32	36
5	0	5	10	15	20	25	30	35	40	45
6	0	6	12	18	24	30	36	42	48	54
7	0	7	14	21	28	35	42	49	56	63
8	0	8	16	24	32	40	48	56	64	72
9	0	9	18	27	36	45	54	63	72	81

● Multiply by 1-Digit Numbers

Multiply 68×6.

Follow these steps:

1. Multiply the ones. Regroup if necessary.

$$\begin{array}{r} 4 \\ 68 \\ \times\ 6 \\ \hline 8 \end{array}$$

8 ones × 6 = 48 ones. Write down the 8, regroup the 4.

2. Multiply the tens. Add the extra 4 tens.

$$\begin{array}{r} 4 \\ 68 \\ \times\ 6 \\ \hline 408 \end{array}$$

6 tens × 6 = 36 tens.
36 tens + 4 tens = 40 tens.

● Multiply by 2-Digit Numbers

To multiply by 2-digit numbers, multiply in 3 steps. First, multiply by the ones. Next, multiply by the tens. Finally, add the **partial products**. Multiply 38×27.

$$\begin{array}{r} 38 \\ \times\ 27 \\ \hline 266 \\ +\ 760 \\ \hline 1,026 \end{array}$$

266 ← Multiply 38 × 7
+ 760 ← Multiply 38 × 20

Do I Understand?

Find the product.

1. 9×5 **2.** 4×7 **3.** $\begin{array}{r} 72 \\ \times\ 9 \end{array}$ **4.** $\begin{array}{r} 43 \\ \times\ 52 \end{array}$

_____   _____

Numbers

A number can be used to tell how many, the order, or to identify.

● Digits

Digits are the symbols used to write numerals: 0, 1, 2, 3, 4, 5, 6, 7, 8, and 9.

● Write Whole Numbers

There are different ways to write **whole numbers**. The number 41,703 can be written in the following ways:

standard form → 41,703

word form → forty-one thousand, seven hundred three

expanded form → 40,000 + 1,000 + 700 + 3

The number 41,703 can also be written in a place-value chart.

Thousands					
Hundreds	Tens	Ones	Hundreds	Tens	Ones
	4	1	7	0	3

● Integers

Integers are all the positive and negative whole numbers. A **negative integer** is written with a negative sign (−) and is to the left of 0 on a number line. A **positive integer** can be written with or without a positive sign (+).

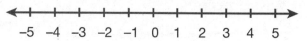

$$-5 \quad -4 \quad -3 \quad -2 \quad -1 \quad 0 \quad 1 \quad 2 \quad 3 \quad 4 \quad 5$$

● Odd and Even Numbers

Odd numbers are those whole numbers that have 1, 3, 5, 7, or 9 in the ones place.

Even numbers are those whole numbers that have 0, 2, 4, 6, or 8 in the ones place.

Even numbers can be divided evenly by 2. Odd numbers cannot.

● Prime and Composite Numbers

A **prime number** is a whole number greater than 1 that has only 1 and itself as factors. Examples of prime numbers include 2, 3, 5, 7, 11, and 13.

A **composite number** is a whole number greater than 1 that has at least 3 factors. Examples of composite numbers include 4, 6, 9, 12, and 15.

Do I Understand?

1. What is 60,000 + 400 + 30 + 7 written in standard form?

_____

2. Is 56 an even or an odd number?

3. Is 37 a prime or composite number?

_____   _____

ANSWERS: 1. 60,437 **2.** even **3.** prime

21

Ordered Pairs

A pair of numbers that gives the location of a point on a graph.

A **coordinate grid** is used to name points on a graph. The points are called **ordered pairs**.

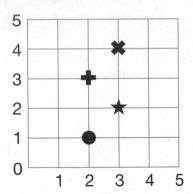

Find the ordered pair of the star.

To read an ordered pair, start at the **origin**, which is located at (0, 0).

The first coordinate names the distance to the right of 0. The star is located 3 units to the right of 0.

The second coordinate names the distance above 0. The star is located 2 units above 0.

The ordered pair for the star is (3, 2).

Perimeter

The distance around the outside of a closed figure.

● How to Find the Perimeter

To find the **perimeter** of a closed figure, add the lengths of each of the sides.

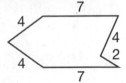

$4 + 4 + 7 + 7 + 4 + 2 = 28$
The perimeter of the figure is 28 units.

● Perimeter of a Rectangle

Formula: $P = (2 \times l) + (2 \times w)$

Multiply the length and width times 2. Then add the products to find the perimeter.

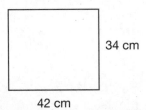

$(2 \times 42) + (2 \times 34) = 84 + 68 = 152$ cm.

The perimeter is 152 cm.

● Perimeter of a Square

To find the perimeter of a square, multiply the length of one of the sides by 4. Formula: $4 \times s$

Find the perimeter of a square with sides of 9 feet.

4×9 ft = 36 ft

The perimeter of the square is 36 feet.

Polygons

A closed figure made of line segments.

● Examples of Polygons

A **polygon** is a closed figure made of line segments. If a figure has a curved side then it is not a polygon. So, a circle is not a polygon. Polygons are **two-dimensional figures**.

triangle	**quadrilateral**	**pentagon**	**hexagon**	**octagon**
3 **sides** and 3 angles	4 sides and 4 angles	5 sides and 5 angles	6 sides and 6 angles	8 sides and 8 angles

● Types of Triangles

Triangles are classified by the number of equal sides and by its angles.

scalene triangle	**isosceles triangle**	**equilateral triangle**
No sides or angles are equal.	At least 2 sides or angles are equal.	3 sides and angles are equal.

  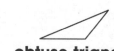

acute triangle	**right triangle**	**obtuse triangle**
All angles are less than 90°.	One angle is a right angle.	One angle is an obtuse angle.

● Types of Quadrilaterals

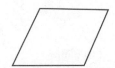

parallelogram	**rhombus**	**rectangle**	**square**	**trapezoid**
both pairs of opposite sides are parallel	parallelogram with all sides the same length	parallelogram with 4 right angles	rectangle with all sides equal	exactly 1 pair of parallel sides

Do I Understand?

1. A triangle has side lengths of 4 cm, 5 cm, and 6 cm. Classify it as *scalene, isosceles,* or *equilateral.*

_____ triangle

23

Probability

The chance that an event will happen.

● Certain, Likely, Unlikely, and Impossible

Probability measures the **chance** of an event happening. An event can be **certain**, **likely**, **unlikely**, or **impossible**.

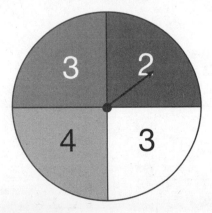

An event that is certain must happen. It is certain that if you spin the spinner you will spin a number less than 5.

A likely event is one that will probably happen, but might not. It is likely that you will spin a 3.

An unlikely event is one that probably will not happen, but could. It is unlikely that you will spin a 2.

An impossible event is one that cannot happen. It is impossible to spin a 1.

● Probability Written as a Fraction

Probability can be written as the following fraction:

$$\frac{\text{the number of favorable outcomes}}{\text{the number of possible outcomes}}$$

The number of **possible outcomes** are each of the possible outcomes. In the bowl of marbles, there are 5 gray, 4 white, and 3 black marbles. There are 12 marbles, so there are 12 possible outcomes. Therefore, 12 is the denominator.

The number of **favorable outcomes** are the desired outcomes. If you wanted to find the probability of picking a white marble, count the number of white marbles. There are 4 white marbles, which is the numerator.

$$\frac{\text{the number of white marbles}}{\text{the total number of marbles}} = \frac{4}{12} = \frac{1}{3}$$

The probability of picking a white marble is $\frac{1}{3}$.

Do I Understand?

Use the spinner.

1. What is the probability of the spinner landing on 2?

_____

Use the bowl of marbles.

2. What is the probability of pulling a black marble?

_____

24

Properties of Addition

The properties of addition can be used to make addition easier. The following properties will also shorten the list of basic facts that need to be memorized.

● Commutative Property
The **commutative property of addition** states that the order of the addends does not change the sum.

$$8 + 7 = 7 + 8$$

● Associative Property
The **associative property of addition** states that the grouping of the addends does not change the sum.

$$6 + (4 + 7) = (6 + 4) + 7$$

● Identity Property
The **identity property of addition** states that when one addend is 0, the sum is equal to the other addend.

$$5 + 0 = 5$$

Properties of Multiplication

The properties of multiplication can be used to make multiplication easier.

● Commutative Property
The **commutative property of multiplication:** the order of the factors does not change the product.

$$8 \times 4 = 4 \times 8$$

● Associative Property
The **associative property of multiplication:** grouping of the factors does not change the product.

$$6 \times (5 \times 9) = (6 \times 5) \times 9$$

● Identity Property
The **identity property of multiplication:** when one factor is 1, the product is equal to the other factor.

$$6 \times 1 = 6$$

● Zero Property
The **zero property of multiplication:** when 0 is multiplied by a number, the product is 0.

$$7 \times 0 = 0$$

● Distributive Property
The **distributive property of multiplication:** to multiply a sum by a number, multiply each addend by the number and add the products.

$$36 \times 8 = (30 \times 8) + (6 \times 8)$$
$$240 \quad + \quad 48 \quad = 288$$

Do I Understand?

1. Use the associative property of addition to find the sum.

$$35 + (65 + 57)$$

_____

Do I Understand?

2. Use the distributive property to find the product of 93×7.

_____

Solid Figures

A figure that has depth.

● Examples of Solid Figures

Solid figures are figures that are not flat. They have depth. Solid figures are called **space figures** or **three-dimensional figures**. Solid figures can be classified by the number of curved surfaces, flat sides, **faces**, **edges**, and **vertices** it has.

A face is a flat surface. An edge is where faces meet. A vertex is where the edges meet. The following solid figures have only flat faces.

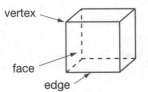
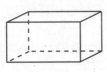
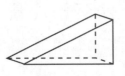

cube	**rectangular prism**	**triangular prism**	**rectangular pyramid**	**triangular pyramid**
6 faces	6 faces	5 faces	5 faces	4 faces
12 edges	12 edges	9 edges	8 edges	6 edges
8 vertices	8 vertices	6 vertices	5 vertices	4 vertices

The solid figures that have curved surfaces are shown below.

cylinder	**cone**	**sphere**
2 flat faces	1 flat face	0 flat faces
1 curved surface	1 curved surface	1 curved surface
2 edges	1 edge	0 edges
0 vertices	1 vertex	0 vertices

Do I Understand?

Zeke

1. Which solid figure has 4 faces?

_____

26

Subtraction

An operation on two numbers that tells how many are left when some are taken away.

● Parts of a Subtraction Problem

These are the parts of a subtraction problem.

$$
\begin{array}{r}
67 \\
- \ 43 \\
\hline
24
\end{array}
$$
← minuend
← subtrahend
← difference

● Subtract Whole Numbers

To subtract whole numbers, subtract from right to left. Regroup if necessary.

Subtract 714 − 336.

$$
\begin{array}{r}
\overset{\overset{10}{6\ \cancel{0}\ 14}}{\cancel{714}} \\
- \ 336 \\
\hline
378
\end{array}
$$

● Subtract Money

Money amounts are also subtracted from right to left.

Subtract $91.27 − $22.79.

$$
\begin{array}{r}
\overset{\overset{10\ \ 11}{8\ \cancel{0}\ \cancel{1}\ 17}}{\$\cancel{91.27}} \\
- \ 22.79 \\
\hline
\$68.48
\end{array}
$$

Remember to include the dollar sign ($) and place the decimal point in the difference.

● Subtract Decimals

Align the digits on the decimal point. There may be a different amount of places after the decimal. If necessary, insert a zero to the end of the decimal. Subtract 72.8 − 57.23.

$$
\begin{array}{r}
\overset{6\ \ 12\ \ 7\ \ 10}{72.8\cancel{0}} \\
- \ 57.23 \\
\hline
15.57
\end{array}
$$

● Subtract Fractions with Like Denominators

Subtract the numerators. The denominator remains the same unless the fraction can be simplified.

$$\frac{11}{12} - \frac{7}{12} = \frac{11-7}{12} = \frac{4}{12} = \frac{1}{3}$$

● Subtract Fractions with Unlike Denominators

Subtract $\frac{3}{4} - \frac{2}{3}$.

First, find the LCD of $\frac{3}{4}$ and $\frac{2}{3}$.

The LCD of $\frac{3}{4}$ and $\frac{2}{3}$ is 12.

Write equivalent fractions using the LCD.

$$\frac{3}{4} = \frac{9}{12} \qquad \frac{2}{3} = \frac{8}{12}$$

Subtract the numerators.

$$\frac{9}{12} - \frac{8}{12} = \frac{1}{12}$$

Do I Understand?

Subtract. For problem 2, write the answer in simplest form.

1. $73.42
   − 58.75

2. $\frac{3}{5} - \frac{1}{2}$

_____   _____

ANSWERS: 1. $14.67 **2.** $\frac{1}{10}$

27

Symmetry

A figure in which both sides of the line match exactly.

● Line of Symmetry

A figure has a **line of symmetry** if it can be folded so that both sides match. Some figures do not have any lines of symmetry. Other figures have more than 1 line of symmetry.

Examples of Lines of Symmetry

  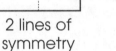 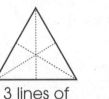

| 0 lines of symmetry | 1 line of symmetry | 2 lines of symmetry | 3 lines of symmetry | 4 lines of symmetry |

Each of the lines creates congruent parts. The figures can be folded along any of those lines and the halves will match exactly.

● Rotational Symmetry

A figure has **rotational symmetry** if it can be turned with a $\frac{1}{2}$ turn or less and have the figure match the original position. For example, a rectangle has rotational symmetry.

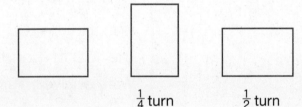

$\frac{1}{4}$ turn $\frac{1}{2}$ turn

As you can see the rectangle after $\frac{1}{2}$ turn looks exactly like it did at the beginning.

Do I Understand?

Use this figure.

1. How many lines of symmetry does the figure have? _____

2. Does the figure have rotational symmetry? _____

28

Temperature

The measure of how hot or cold something is.

● Measure Temperature

In the United States, **temperature** is usually measured in **degrees Fahrenheit (°F)**. In most of the rest of the world temperature is measured in **degrees Celsius (°C)**. To read a **thermometer**, look at where the liquid inside the thermometer stops. This tells the temperature.

Fahrenheit

240°F
220°F ← 212°F Water Boils
200°F
180°F
160°F
140°F
120°F
100°F ← 98.6°F Normal body temperature
80°F ← 68°F Room temperature
60°F
40°F ← 32°F Water freezes
20°F
0°F
–10°F

Celsius

120°C
110°C
100°C ← 100°C Water Boils
90°C
80°C
70°C
60°C
50°C
40°C ← 37°C Normal body temperature
30°C
20°C ← 20°C Room temperature
10°C
0°C ← 0°C Water freezes
–10°C

● Estimate Between °F and °C

If the temperature is 20°C, you can estimate the temperature in °F by following these steps:

1. To estimate, double the °C temperature. $20 \times 2 = 40$

2. Add 30. $40 + 30 = 70$

The temperature is about 70°F.

Do I Understand?

1. What is the difference between room temperature and the temperature at which water freezes in degrees Celsius?

_____ °C

2. If the temperature is 12°C, what is an estimate of the temperature in °F?

_____ °F

ANSWERS: 1. 20 2. about 54

29

Time

A way to keep track of when something occurs.

● Tell Time

A clock has a minute hand and an hour hand. The shorter hand is the hour hand. The longer hand is the minute hand. The clock reads 5:15.

● A.M. and P.M.

A.M. names the times of the day from 12 midnight until 12 noon.

P.M. names the times of the day from 12 noon until 12 midnight.

Units of Time		
1 **minute (min)**	=	60 **seconds (s)**
$\frac{1}{4}$ **hour (h)**	=	15 min
$\frac{1}{2}$ hour	=	30 min
1 hour	=	60 min
1 **day (d)**	=	24 h

Greater Units of Time		
1 **week (wk)**	=	7 d
1 **month** is about		30 d
1 **year (y)**	=	12 mo or 365 d
1 **leap year**	=	366 d

● Elapsed Time

Elapsed time is the measure of how much time passed from the start of an event to the end of an event. For example, Marco went to school at 7:45 A.M. He returned home at 3:15 P.M. How long was Marco away from home?

To find elapsed time when changing from A.M. to P.M. or P.M. to A.M., follow these steps:

1. Count the minutes until the next hour.
   7:45 A.M. to 8:00 A.M. is 15 minutes.

2. Count the hours until the end of the event.
   8:00 A.M. to 3:00 P.M. is 7 hours.

3. Count the minutes until the end of the event.
   3:00 P.M. to 3:15 P.M. is 15 minutes.

4. Add the time in steps 1–3.
   15 min + 7 h + 15 min = 7 h 30 min

Marco was away from home for 7 hours 30 minutes.

Do I Understand?

Use the clock at right.

1. What time does the clock show? _____

2. What time was it 3 hours 40 minutes before the time on the clock? _____

30

Transformations

The movement of a figure.

● Translations

A **translation**, or slide, moves a figure along a line.

● Reflections

A **reflection**, or flip, produces a mirror image of a figure.

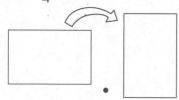

● Rotations

A **rotation**, or turn, turns a figure around a point. This rectangle has been turned $\frac{1}{4}$ turn.

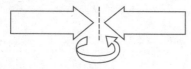

● What Happens

The shape and size of a figure do not change when the figure is slid, flipped, or turned. The figures are congruent.

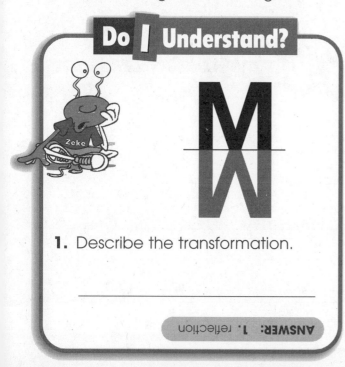

Do I Understand?

1. Describe the transformation.

_____

Volume

The amount of space a solid figure encloses, measured in cubic units.

● Volume of a Prism

Volume is the product of the measure of three dimensions: length, width, and height. Volume is measured in **cubic units**. Cubic units can be in any measure of length. For example, cubic centimeters can be written as cm^3.

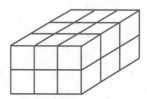

To find volume, count the number of cubes in each layer. There are 9 cubes in each layer: $9 + 9 = 18$ cubes

Multiplication can be used to find the volume. Multiply the length times the width times the height.

Volume = length × width × height

$V = l \times w \times h$
$V = 3 \times 3 \times 2$
$V = 18$ cubic units

Do I Understand?

1. What is the volume of a box with a length of 7 in., a width of 4 in., and a height of 3 in.?

_____ in.^{3}

Glossary

acute angle An angle less than a right angle. *(p. 5)*

acute triangle A triangle with 3 acute angles. *(p. 23)*

addend A number to be added; Ex. In 7 + 5 = 12, 7 and 5 are the addends. *(p. 3)*

addition (+) An operation on two or more numbers to find a sum. *(p. 3)*

A.M. A name for the time between 12 midnight and 12 noon. *(p. 30)*

angle A figure formed when two rays meet at the same endpoint. *(p. 5)*

area The number of square units needed to cover a region. *(p. 6)*

associative property of addition The grouping of the addends does not change the sum.
Ex. 4 + (6 + 8) = (4 + 6) + 8 *(p. 25)*

associative property of multiplication The grouping of the factors does not change the product.
Ex. 4 × (5 × 7) = (4 × 5) × 7 *(p. 25)*

average The sum of the addends divided by the number of addends; Also known as the mean. *(p. 7)*

bar graph A graph that shows data by using bars of different lengths. *(p. 16)*

capacity The amount a container can hold. *(p. 19)*

center The point that is the same distance from all points on a circle. *(p. 8)*

centimeter (cm) A metric unit of length; 1 centimeter = 10 millimeters. See chart. *(p. 19)*

certain An event that must happen. *(p. 24)*

chance The likeliness of an event happening. *(p. 24)*

My Math Words

chord Any line segment that connects two points on a circle. *(p. 8)*

circle A plane figure having all points the same distance from a fixed point called the center. *(p. 8)*

circle graph A graph that shows data by using parts of a circle. *(p. 17)*

commutative property of addition The order of the addends does not change the sum.
Ex. $8 + 9 = 9 + 8$ *(p. 25)*

commutative property of multiplication The order of the factors does not change the product.
Ex. $8 \times 6 = 6 \times 8$ *(p. 25)*

compatible numbers Numbers that are easy to compute with mentally. *(p. 13)*

composite number A number with more than 1 and itself as factors.
Ex. 4, 6, 9, 10 *(p. 21)*

cone A pointed solid figure with a circular base. *(p. 26)*

congruent figures Figures that have the same shape and size. *(p. 10)*

coordinate grid A graph used to show location of points by using ordered pairs. *(p. 22)*

cube A solid figure with 6 square faces. *(p. 26)*

cubic units The volume of a cube, one of whose sides is the given unit of length. *(p. 31)*

cup (c) A customary unit of capacity; 1 cup = 8 fluid ounces. See chart. *(p. 19)*

cylinder A solid figure with 2 congruent faces that are circular. *(p. 26)*

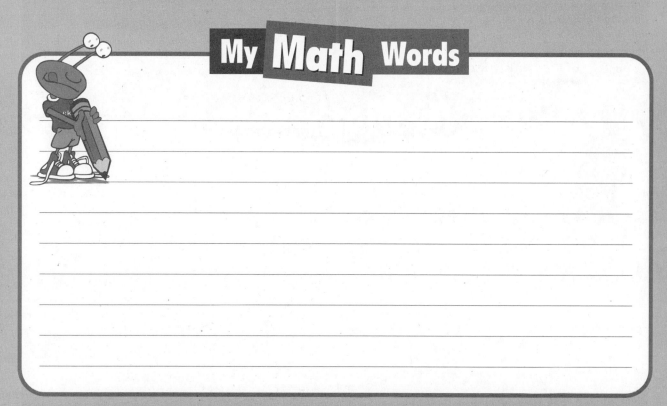

My Math Words

Glossary

data Information (p. 7)

day A period of time; 1 day = 24 hours. (p. 30)

decimal A number with a decimal point in it. Ex. 2.75, 0.4 (p. 11)

decimal point (.) A period separating the ones from the tenths in a decimal. (p. 11)

degree (°) Unit used for measuring angles. (p. 5)

degrees Celsius (°C) Unit for measuring temperature. See chart. (p. 29)

degrees Fahrenheit (°F) Unit for measuring temperature. See chart. (p. 29)

denominator The number below the bar in a fraction. It tells how many equal parts in all. Ex. In $\frac{2}{3}$, 3 is the denominator. (p. 15)

diameter A chord that passes through the center of a circle. (p. 8)

difference The answer to a subtraction problem. Ex. In 8 − 3 = 5, 5 is the difference. (p. 27)

digit Any of the symbols used to write numbers. The digits are 0, 1, 2, 3, 4, 5, 6, 7, 8, and 9. (p. 21)

distributive property of multiplication To multiply a sum by a number, you can multiply each addend by the number and add the products. Ex. 23 × 6 = (20 × 6) + (3 × 6) (p. 25)

dividend A number to be divided. Ex. In 12 ÷ 4 = 3, 12 is the dividend. (p. 12)

division (÷) An operation on two numbers that tells how many groups or how many in each group. (p. 12)

divisor The number by which the dividend is divided. Ex. In 12 ÷ 4 = 3, 4 is the divisor. (p. 12)

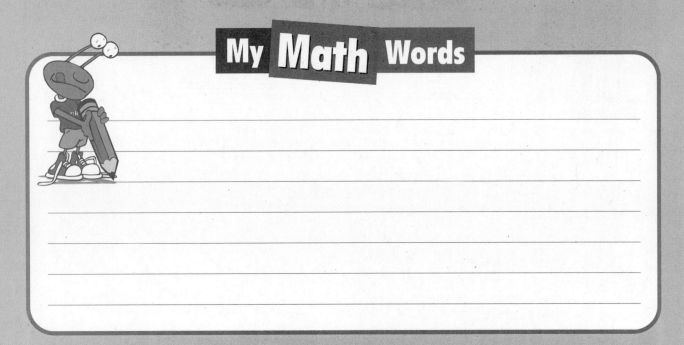

My Math Words

edge A line segment where two faces of a solid figure meet. *(p. 26)*

elapsed time The time from the start of an event until the end of an event. *(p. 30)*

equation A number sentence that shows that 2 amounts are equal. *(p. 4)*

equilateral triangle A triangle with 3 sides the same length. *(p. 23)*

equivalent fractions Two or more different fractions that name the same amount. *(p. 15)*

estimate An answer close to the exact answer. *(p. 13)*

even number A number that has 0, 2, 4, 6, or 8 in the ones place. *(p. 21)*

expanded form The sum of the values of each of the digits in a number. Ex. 3,926 = 3,000 + 900 + 20 + 6 *(p. 21)*

expression A group of numbers and symbols that shows a mathematical quantity. Ex. 2 + x, 4 − 3 *(p. 4)*

face A flat side of a solid figure. *(p. 26)*

factors Numbers that are multiplied to give a product. Ex. In 4 × 5 = 20, 4 and 5 are the factors. *(p. 14)*

favorable outcomes The desired outcomes of a probability experiment. *(p. 24)*

fluid ounce (fl oz) A customary unit of capacity; 8 fluid ounces = 1 cup. See chart. *(p. 19)*

foot (ft) A customary unit of length; 1 foot = 12 inches. See chart. *(p. 19)*

fraction A number that names part of a whole or a group. Ex. $\frac{1}{2}$, $\frac{3}{4}$ *(p. 15)*

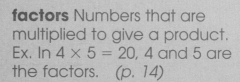
My **Math** Words

_____
_____
_____
_____
_____
_____
_____
_____

Glossary

gallon (gal) A customary unit of capacity; 1 gallon = 4 quarts. See chart. *(p. 19)*

gram (g) A metric unit of mass; 1 gram = 1,000 milligrams. See chart. *(p. 19)*

greatest common factor (GCF) The greatest factor that is common to two or more numbers. Ex. 4 is the GCF of 8 and 12. *(p. 14)*

hexagon A polygon with 6 sides. *(p. 23)*

hour (h) A period of time; 1 hour = 60 minutes. *(p. 30)*

hundredth A decimal place equal to 0.01. *(p. 11)*

identity property of addition When one addend is 0, the sum is the same as the other addend. Ex. 8 + 0 = 8 *(p. 25)*

identity property of multiplication When one factor is 1, the product is the same as the other factor. Ex. $5 \times 1 = 5$ *(p. 25)*

impossible An event that cannot happen. *(p. 24)*

inch (in.) A customary unit of length; 12 inches = 1 foot. See chart. *(p. 19)*

integer All the positive and negative whole numbers and 0. *(p. 21)*

intersecting lines Lines that meet or cross each other. *(p. 18)*

interval The difference between numbers on an axis of a graph. *(p. 16)*

inverse operations Operations that are opposites, such as addition and subtraction, and multiplication and division. *(p. 4)*

is equal to (=) A symbol used to show that two quantities have the same value. *(p. 8)*

is greater than (>) Symbol to show that the first number is greater than the second number. *(p. 8)*

is less than (<) A symbol used to show that the first number is less than the second number. *(p. 8)*

isosceles triangle A triangle with at least 2 equal sides. *(p. 23)*

My Math Words

key In a pictograph, the key tells how many items each symbol represents. *(p. 16)*

kilogram (kg) A metric unit of mass; 1 kilogram = 1,000 grams. See chart. *(p. 19)*

kilometer (km) A metric unit of length; 1 kilometer = 1,000 meters. See chart. *(p. 19)*

least common denominator (LCD) The least common multiple of two or more denominators. Ex. The LCD of $\frac{2}{3}$ and $\frac{3}{4}$ is 12. *(p. 9)*

least common multiple (LCM) The least whole number greater than 0, that is a multiple of each of two or more numbers. Ex. The LCM of 4 and 6 is 12. *(p. 14)*

length The measurement between two endpoints. *(p. 19)*

like denominators Denominators that are the same number. *(p. 3)*

likely An event that will probably happen, but might not. *(p. 24)*

line A straight path that goes in two directions forever without end. *(p. 18)*

line graph A graph that uses a line to show how something changes over time. *(p. 17)*

line of symmetry A line on which a figure can be folded so that both sides match. *(p. 28)*

line segment A part of a line with two endpoints. *(p. 18)*

liter (L) A metric unit of capacity; 1 liter = 1,000 milliliters. See chart. *(p. 19)*

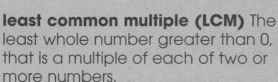

My Math Words

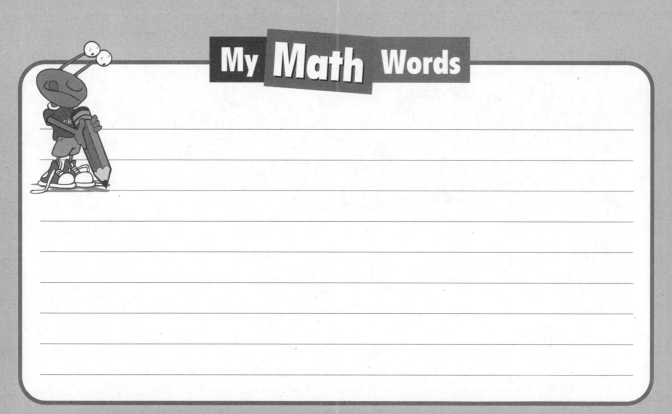

Glossary

mass The amount of matter in an object. *(p. 19)*

mean The sum of the addends divided by the number of addends. Also known as the average. *(p. 7)*

median The middle number in an ordered group of numbers. *(p. 7)*

meter (m) A metric unit of length; 1 meter = 100 centimeters. See chart. *(p. 19)*

mile (mi) A customary unit of length; 1 mile = 5,280 feet. See chart. *(p. 19)*

milligram (mg) A metric unit of mass; 1,000 milligrams = 1 gram. See chart. *(p. 19)*

milliliter (mL) A metric unit of capacity; 1,000 milliliters = 1 liter. See chart. *(p. 19)*

millimeter (mm) A metric unit of length; 10 millimeters = 1 centimeter. See chart. *(p. 19)*

minuend The number from which the subtrahend is subtracted. Ex. In 9 − 3 = 6, 9 is the minuend. *(p. 27)*

mixed number A number that has a whole-number part and a fraction part. Ex. $2\frac{3}{5}$ *(p. 15)*

mode The number that occurs the most in a set of data. *(p. 7)*

month (mo) A period of time from 28 to 31 days. See chart. *(p. 30)*

multiple The product of a number and any whole number. Ex. The multiples of 3 include 3, 6, 9. *(p. 14)*

multiplication (×) A shortcut for repeated addition. *(p. 20)*

negative integer An integer less than 0. *(p. 21)*

numerator The number above the bar in a fraction. It tells how many parts are being considered. Ex. In $\frac{3}{4}$, 3 is the numerator. *(p. 15)*

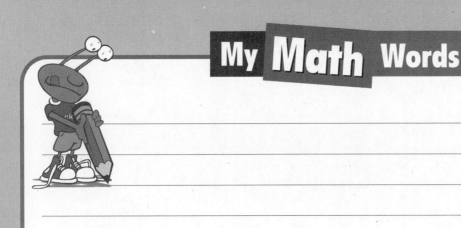

My Math Words

38

O

obtuse angle An angle greater than a right angle. (*p. 5*)

obtuse triangle A triangle with one obtuse angle. (*p. 23*)

octagon A polygon with 8 sides. (*p. 23*)

odd number A number with 1, 3, 5, 7, or 9 in the ones place. (*p. 21*)

ordered pair A pair of numbers that gives the location of a point on a graph. (*p. 22*)

origin The point of a coordinate grid where the horizontal and vertical axes meet, known as (0, 0). (*p. 22*)

ounce (oz) A customary unit of weight; 16 ounces = 1 pound. See chart. (*p. 19*)

P

parallel lines Lines that stay the same distance apart and never meet. (*p. 18*)

parallelogram A quadrilateral with both pairs of opposite sides parallel. (*p. 23*)

partial product The product of each part of a multiplication problem when multiplying by 2-digit factors or more. (*p. 20*)

pentagon A polygon with 5 sides. (*p. 23*)

per For each. (*p. 7*)

perimeter The distance around the outside of a closed figure. (*p. 22*)

perpendicular lines Lines that meet or cross at a right angle. (*p. 18*)

pictograph A graph that shows data by using symbols. (*p. 16*)

My Math Words

Glossary

pint (pt) A customary unit of capacity; 1 pint = 2 cups. See chart. *(p. 19)*

P.M. A name for the time from 12 noon to 12 midnight. *(p. 30)*

polygon A closed figure made of line segments. *(p. 23)*

positive integer An integer greater than 0. *(p. 21)*

possible outcomes Any of the results that could happen in an experiment. *(p. 24)*

pound (lb) A customary unit of weight; 1 pound = 16 ounces. See chart. *(p. 19)*

prime number A number with only 1 and itself as factors. Ex. 2, 3, 5, 7 *(p. 21)*

probability The chance that an event will occur. *(p. 24)*

product The answer to a multiplication problem. Ex. In 8 × 4 = 32, 32 is the product. *(p. 20)*

protractor A tool used to measure angles. *(p. 5)*

quadrilateral A polygon with 4 sides. *(p. 23)*

quart (qt) A customary unit of capacity; 1 quart = 2 pints. See chart. *(p. 19)*

quotient The answer to a division problem. Ex. In 16 ÷ 8 = 2, 2 is the quotient. *(p. 12)*

radius A line segment from the center of a circle to any point on the circle. *(p. 8)*

range The least number subtracted from the greatest number in a data set. *(p. 7)*

ray A part of a line with one endpoint and which goes on forever in one direction. *(p. 18)*

rectangle A parallelogram with 4 right angles. *(p. 23)*

rectangular prism A solid figure with 6 faces, 12 edges, and 8 vertices. *(p. 26)*

My Math Words

rectangular pyramid A solid figure with 5 faces, 8 edges, and 5 vertices. (p. 26)

reflection The movement of a figure across a line producing a mirror image. (p. 31)

regroup To rename a number. Ex. 17 can be renamed as 1 ten and 7 ones. (p. 3)

regular polygon A polygon with all sides and angles equal. (p. 10)

remainder A number less than the divisor that remains after division has ended.
Ex. In 23 ÷ 3 = 7 R2, 2 is the remainder. (p. 11)

rhombus A parallelogram with 4 equal sides. (p. 23)

right angle An angle that forms a square corner. (p. 5)

right triangle A triangle that has one right angle. (p. 23)

rotation Turns a figure around a point. (p. 31)

rotational symmetry
A figure that matches itself after $\frac{1}{2}$ turn or less. (p. 28)

round To find the value of a number based on a given place value. (p. 13)

scalene triangle A triangle that does not have equal sides or angles. (p. 23)

second (s) A unit of time; 60 seconds = 1 minute. See chart. (p. 30)

side One of the line segments of a polygon. (p. 23)

similar figures Figures that have the same shape but may have different sizes. (p. 10)

simplest form A fraction whose numerator and denominator have only 1 as a common factor. (p. 15)

solid figure Any figure that has depth. (p. 26)

My Math Words

Glossary

space figure Another name for a solid figure.   (p. 26)

sphere A solid figure that has the shape of a ball.   (p. 26)

square A rectangle with 4 equal sides. (p. 23)

square numbers The product of two factors that are the same.
Ex. 9 is a square number because $3 \times 3 = 9$.   (p. 14)

square units The area of a square, one of whose sides is the given unit of length.   (p. 6)

standard form A way of writing a number using only digits.   (p. 21)

straight angle An angle that forms a straight line.   (p. 5)

subtraction (−) An operation on two numbers that tells how many are left when some are taken away.   (p. 27)

subtrahend The number that is subtracted from the minuend.
Ex. In $11 - 5 = 6$, 5 is the subtrahend. (p. 27)

sum The answer to an addition problem.
Ex. In $7 + 4 = 11$, 11 is the sum.   (p. 3)

temperature A measurement that tells how hot or cold something is.   (p. 29)

tenth A decimal place equal to 0.1.   (p. 11)

thermometer An instrument used to tell temperature.   (p. 29)

thousandth A decimal place equal to 0.001.   (p. 11)

three-dimensional figure Another name for a solid figure.   (p. 26)

ton (T) A customary unit of weight; 1 ton = 2,000 pounds. See chart. (p. 19)

transformation The movement of a figure.   (p. 31)

translation To move a figure along a line.   (p. 31)

trapezoid A quadrilateral with exactly 1 pair of parallel sides.   (p. 23)

triangle A polygon with 3 sides. (p. 23)

triangular prism A solid figure with 5 faces, 9 edges, and 6 vertices. (p. 26)

My Math Words

triangular pyramid A solid figure with 4 faces, 6 edges, and 4 vertices. *(p. 26)*

two-dimensional figure A figure that has only length and width. Circles and polygons are two-dimensional figures. *(p. 23)*

unlikely An event that probably will not happen, but could. *(p. 24)*

variable A letter or symbol used to represent a number. Ex. In $3 + x = 5$, x is the variable. *(p. 4)*

vertex The point where the rays meet in an angle. *(p. 5)*
The point where 3 or more edges meet in a solid figure. *(p. 26)*

volume The amount of space that a solid figure encloses. *(p. 31)*

week (wk) A period of time; 1 week = 7 days. *(p. 30)*

weight A measurement that tells how heavy an object is. *(p. 19)*

whole number The numbers 0, 1, 2, 3, etc. *(p. 21)*

word form A way of writing a number using words. Ex. In word form, 3,681 is written as three thousand, six hundred eighty-one. *(p. 21)*

yard (yd) A customary unit of length; 1 yard = 3 feet. See chart. *(p. 19)*

year (y) A period of time equal to 365 days. A leap year is equal to 366 days. *(p. 30)*

zero property of multiplication When zero is one of the factors, the product is 0. Ex. $9 \times 0 = 0$ *(p. 25)*

My Math Words

Fun Facts!

Addition

1. 1 + 6
2. 6 + 9
3. 4 + 4
4. 2 + 7
5. 7 + 7
6. 7 + 4

7. 4 + 2
8. 8 + 9
9. 5 + 7
10. 6 + 5
11. 6 + 6
12. 3 + 6

13. 6 + 2
14. 3 + 3
15. 5 + 5
16. 3 + 9
17. 9 + 9
18. 3 + 8

19. 8 + 5
20. 9 + 1
21. 7 + 8
22. 9 + 5
23. 3 + 4
24. 2 + 9

25. 2 + 2
26. 4 + 1
27. 7 + 1
28. 2 + 8
29. 6 + 7
30. 8 + 8

Subtraction

1. 6 − 2
2. 6 − 3
3. 12 − 3
4. 7 − 5
5. 18 − 9
6. 16 − 8

7. 13 − 7
8. 9 − 8
9. 11 − 8
10. 17 − 8
11. 9 − 4
12. 10 − 6

13. 12 − 8
14. 13 − 9
15. 10 − 8
16. 7 − 2
17. 15 − 5
18. 10 − 5

19. 14 − 6
20. 9 − 5
21. 11 − 7
22. 12 − 7
23. 5 − 3
24. 8 − 4

25. 17 − 9
26. 15 − 9
27. 14 − 7
28. 8 − 3
29. 10 − 4
30. 15 − 6

Fun Facts!

Multiplication

1.	8 × 5	**2.**	7 × 7	**3.**	5 × 9	**4.**	2 × 7	**5.**	1 × 7	**6.**	8 × 7
7.	4 × 2	**8.**	3 × 3	**9.**	0 × 6	**10.**	4 × 3	**11.**	6 × 9	**12.**	7 × 5
13.	5 × 5	**14.**	8 × 9	**15.**	2 × 8	**16.**	9 × 3	**17.**	6 × 6	**18.**	8 × 8
19.	4 × 4	**20.**	4 × 1	**21.**	6 × 2	**22.**	5 × 6	**23.**	6 × 7	**24.**	2 × 9
25.	2 × 2	**26.**	9 × 9	**27.**	9 × 1	**28.**	3 × 8	**29.**	3 × 6	**30.**	7 × 4

Division

1.	36 ÷ 6	**2.**	35 ÷ 7	**3.**	28 ÷ 4	**4.**	18 ÷ 6	**5.**	63 ÷ 9	**6.**	16 ÷ 4
7.	45 ÷ 5	**8.**	24 ÷ 8	**9.**	42 ÷ 7	**10.**	14 ÷ 2	**11.**	27 ÷ 3	**12.**	30 ÷ 5
13.	49 ÷ 7	**14.**	81 ÷ 9	**15.**	20 ÷ 4	**16.**	40 ÷ 8	**17.**	24 ÷ 4	**18.**	21 ÷ 7
19.	56 ÷ 7	**20.**	12 ÷ 3	**21.**	15 ÷ 5	**22.**	36 ÷ 9	**23.**	12 ÷ 6	**24.**	16 ÷ 2
25.	72 ÷ 8	**26.**	25 ÷ 5	**27.**	54 ÷ 9	**28.**	48 ÷ 6	**29.**	18 ÷ 9	**30.**	32 ÷ 4

Answers to Fun Facts!

Addition

1. 7	**2.** 15	**3.** 8	**4.** 9	**5.** 14	**6.** 11
7. 6	**8.** 17	**9.** 12	**10.** 11	**11.** 12	**12.** 9
13. 8	**14.** 6	**15.** 10	**16.** 12	**17.** 18	**18.** 11
19. 13	**20.** 10	**21.** 15	**22.** 14	**23.** 7	**24.** 11
25. 4	**26.** 5	**27.** 8	**28.** 10	**29.** 13	**30.** 16

Subtraction

1. 4	**2.** 3	**3.** 9	**4.** 2	**5.** 9	**6.** 8
7. 6	**8.** 1	**9.** 3	**10.** 9	**11.** 5	**12.** 4
13. 4	**14.** 4	**15.** 2	**16.** 5	**17.** 10	**18.** 5
19. 8	**20.** 4	**21.** 4	**22.** 5	**23.** 2	**24.** 4
25. 8	**26.** 6	**27.** 7	**28.** 5	**29.** 6	**30.** 9

Multiplication

1. 40	**2.** 49	**3.** 45	**4.** 14	**5.** 7	**6.** 56
7. 8	**8.** 9	**9.** 0	**10.** 12	**11.** 54	**12.** 35
13. 25	**14.** 72	**15.** 16	**16.** 27	**17.** 36	**18.** 64
19. 16	**20.** 4	**21.** 12	**22.** 30	**23.** 42	**24.** 18
25. 4	**26.** 81	**27.** 9	**28.** 24	**29.** 18	**30.** 28

Division

1. 6	**2.** 5	**3.** 7	**4.** 3	**5.** 7	**6.** 4
7. 9	**8.** 3	**9.** 6	**10.** 7	**11.** 9	**12.** 6
13. 7	**14.** 9	**15.** 5	**16.** 5	**17.** 6	**18.** 3
19. 8	**20.** 4	**21.** 3	**22.** 4	**23.** 2	**24.** 8
25. 9	**26.** 5	**27.** 6	**28.** 8	**29.** 2	**30.** 8

Math **Abbreviations**

centimeter	cm	**hour**	h	**liter**	L	**pint**	pt
cup	c	**inch**	in.	**meter**	m	**pound**	lb
day	d	**kilogram**	kg	**mile**	mi	**quart**	qt
fluid ounce	fl oz	**kilometer**	km	**milligram**	mg	**second**	s
foot	ft	**least common denominator**	LCD	**milliliter**	mL	**ton**	T
gallon	gal			**millimeter**	mm	**week**	wk
gram	g	**least common multiple**	LCM	**minute**	min	**yard**	yd
greatest common factor	GCF			**month**	mo	**year**	y
				ounce	oz		

Time **Measurements**

Days of the Week	Months of the Year	Days in Month
Sunday	January	31
Monday	February	28 or 29
Tuesday	March	31
Wednesday	April	30
Thursday	May	31
Friday	June	30
Saturday	July	31
	August	31
	September	30
	October	31
	November	30
	December	31

Larger **Units of Time**

1 week (wk)	=	7 days
1 month (mo)	is about	30 days
1 year (y)	=	12 months or 365 days
1 year	is about	52 weeks
1 leap year	=	366 days
1 decade	=	10 years
1 century	=	100 years

Math **Symbols**

+	addition		"	inches
+3	positive 3		'	feet
−	subtraction		°	degree
−3	negative 3		°C	degrees Celsius
×	multiplication		°F	degrees Fahrenheit
÷	division			line $\overleftrightarrow{AB}$
$\overline{)}$	division			ray $\overrightarrow{AB}$
=	is equal to		$\overline{AB}$	line segment $\overline{AB}$
>	is greater than		∠A	angle *A*
<	is less than		∟	right angle
.	decimal point		△ABC	triangle *ABC*
$	dollars		⊥	perpendicular lines
¢	cents		‖	parallel
(2, 3)	ordered pair (2, 3)		~	approximately

Math **Formulas**

Perimeter of a rectangle	$P = 2l + 2w$
Perimeter of a square	$P = 4s$
Area of a rectangle	$A = lw$
Volume of a prism	$V = lwh$
Probability	$P = \dfrac{\text{number of favorable outcomes}}{\text{number of possible outcomes}}$